The Historical Development of Legal Apologetics

With an Emphasis on the Resurrection

By

William P. Broughton

PRESS

Contents

Preface.. vii

1. An Introduction..11

2. Development of Apologetics during the
    New Testament and Early Patristic Era 21

3. Development of Apologetics from
    Augustine to the Reformation..........................31

4. Development of Apologetics during the
    Reformation and the Enlightenment...............37

5. Development of Apologetics in the
    Nineteenth and Early Twentieth Centuries 55

6. The Characteristics of Contemporary
    Legal Apologetics 67

7. The Legal Apologetic's Classification
    Status and Distinctive Features.......................83

8. The Central Divide in Contemporary
   Apologetics 89

9. The Relevance and Effectiveness of
   Legal Apologetics 109

   Glossary of Terms *123*

Preface

When I enrolled at Trinity Theological Seminary for my Doctor of Ministry degree in1998, one of the first things I was asked to do was to read John Warwick Montgomery's book titled *Faith Founded on Fact*. I found this book very interesting; but more than that, it grabbed my attention because I discovered that Montgomery uses evidential apologetics in explaining the facticity of the resurrection of Jesus, as well as the other miracles mentioned in the Scriptures. I had been exposed to many other notions concerning the resurrection, but none of these discussions fully convinced me of the credibility of the miracle accounts in the Gospels. The scholars in the early twentieth century called the miracles myths, which were written by well-meaning but misguided people. These notions were passed on to me in my prior seminary training.

I remember in my first pastorate that I was left in a state of confusion on how to approach the Scriptures, especially the accounts of the resurrection of Jesus. Were the accounts true as they are written, or should we accept the theological reasoning of the various liberal scholars? Montgomery says in his preface *to Faith Founded on Fact,* "A non-evidential apologetic is a contradiction in terms." This statement brought many of my earlier beliefs concerning the resurrection into focus since I find concrete facts more convincing than metaphysical arguments. Another pastor once confessed that he often wondered whether or not what he told his parishioners on Sunday mornings was true. I shared the same dilemma from time to time in my own ministry and wished that I had studied a course in evidential apologetics. Unfortunately in the 1980s no such course was offered in many seminaries, including my own.

After reading Montgomery's book, I wanted to hear more about apologetics and the reasoning ability of Dr. Montgomery, so I purchased many of his lecture tapes, especially those concerning the case for evidence in evaluating the New Testament accounts of the miracles of Jesus, particularly His resurrection. It was because of these lectures that I became interested in the evidential and legal methods of doing apologetics. As a result I have established a substantial apologetic library of my own, representing many schools of apologetics. Many of these resources were used as source material and inspiration in writing this book.

The reader will no doubt see that *Faith Founded on Fact* and Ross Clifford's book titled *John Warwick Montgomery's Legal Apologetic* were both strong influences in the writing of this book. As a result of my own study, many doubts have been clarified for me, and I commend the legal apologetic system to the reader. It is my hope that the discussion in this book will help you in deciding on an apologetic system for your own use and clarify any doubts you may have concerning the Christian faith.

I would like to thank my wife, Bonnie, for her loving patience during the time I have spent composing this book. Also thanks to my former professor of systematic theology Dr. Clark Pinnock (now Emeritus Professor) at McMaster Divinity College, in Hamilton, Ontario. He taught me to appreciate the study of theology and Christian interpretation and has read through the manuscript and made some gracious comments. I would also like to thank some of the parishioners in my church who struggled through the manuscript and gave me some insight as to how the general reader would view this work. I would also like to thank Jarl Waggoner, my editor, who reviewed the manuscript and made this book more readable. It is my hope that the Word of God will be further understood after reading the contents of this book.

1

An Introduction

Background

Montgomery: The Leading Apologist of Our Time

Since the publication of John Warwick Montgomery's book *The Law above the Law* (1975),[1] there has been a continual rise in the use of legal concepts and methods within the field of Christian apologetics and is especially true in the defense of the historical soundness of Jesus' resurrection. As Montgomery often has said himself, the use of legal principles, procedures, and standards to evaluate Christian evidence for the resurrection did not originate with him.[2] For example, in the early seventeenth century, Hugo Grotius, the "father of international law" and the first Protestant apologete, wrote *The Truth of the Christian Religion* (1627).[3] In this work he provided us with a legal argument for the authenticity of the New Testament and its "admissibility" as a piece of evidence in a hypothetical court of law. This also acted as an affirmative proof of the resurrection, which is based upon the testimonies of the first-century eyewitnesses to the risen Christ.

We know that Montgomery's legal apologetic is strongly influenced by the nineteenth-century American legal scholar Simon Greenleaf and his book *The Testimony of the Evangelists*[4] because the book is included and revised as an appendix in Montgomery's book, *The Law above the Law*. Although Montgomery deserves recognition for identifying these works as foundational to a legal apologetic, he did not rediscover a method of identifying evidences for the resurrection. I say this because a century before *The Law above the Law* came into print, Francis Wharton noted that Christian apologists have at all times used juridical tests, or at least appealed to juridical standards in the process of practicing their craft.[5] In support of this contention and its extension into our own age, it has been said that "since the seventeenth century, over one hundred and twenty Christian apologists have composed juridical or legally styled apologetic texts."[6] The majority of these authors apparently have focused on gathering evidence for the resurrection, and during the past three decades or so the use of a juridical model has "flourished."[7]

Why Montgomery's Apologetic Is Significant Today

By any measure, John Warwick Montgomery is now the most significant supporter of the legal or juridical apologetic for the resurrection of Jesus. Increasing interest in this approach has been driven, to some extent, by his labors and the positive reception they have received from evidential apologists in the United States and Great Britain.[8] The impact of Montgomery's work also has been enlarged by his credentials as a "renowned theologian, philosopher and lawyer."[9] Not only does Montgomery hold ten advanced degrees (three of them in jurisprudence),[10] but he is also an extraordinarily prolific author. Since the late 1950s, he has written over forty full-length texts and literally hundreds of essays and articles.[11] His first major apologetic appeared in 1964 under the title of *History and Christianity*,[12] which was composed in an easy-to-understand style aimed at a general readership. The arguments he presented in that text were subsequently spread by Josh McDowell through Campus Crusade in the early 1970s.[13] This exposure added to Montgomery's growing reputation and influence. Finally, Montgomery took the leading role in the establishment of the Simon Greenleaf School of Law (renamed Trinity Law School), creating an institutional setting within which a "new generation of apologists can interact with the legal method."[14]

Presentation of this Discussion

What is Legal Apologetics?

Montgomery's career as a practitioner of legal apologetics emerged from his initial use of a historical defense for the resurrection. His intimate familiarity with common-law doctrine naturally led to a shift toward a clearly juridical model. Therefore, legal apologetics constitutes a distinct phase in the work of its leading contemporary advocate. Nevertheless, the nature and status of the legal approach to Christian apologetics is not entirely clear. Some have described legal apologetics as a "genre" and then designated it as an "apologetic school" because it has "become so broadly based and dominant."[15] This broader status as a "school" is closely related to the historical argument for the resurrection of Jesus; however legal apologetics does have its own characteristics.[16] Juridical, or legal, apologetics may be defined as an apologetic *style* that "employs either general legal principles or technical legal criteria in presenting a reasoned case for Christian belief."[17] Some also have elevated this "style" into a "distinct school."[18] But does the legal apologetic embodied, *among other things*, in the works of John Warwick Montgomery, constitute a full-fledged school? Any attempt to develop even a short-term answer to this question solely on the basis of standard overviews and histories of Christian apologetics would yield a negative finding or, more precisely, no finding at all. In the preface to his inventory of juridical apologetes, Philip Johnson says that, "remarkably, their contributions as a distinct school had gone unrecognized in the introductory textbooks on apologetics, even when such texts occasionally mention one or more legal apologists."[19]

The Need for Clarification

The best-known historical study of Christian apologetics, *A History of Apologetics* by Avery Dulles, includes only a brief section about Hugo Grotius's work, *The Truth of the Christian Religion,* and only a casual reference to Thomas Sherlock's *The Tryal of the Witnesses of the Resurrection of Jesus.*[20] Furthermore, Dulles's text is devoid of any reference to Simon Greenleaf. More recently, Kenneth Boa and Robert M. Bowman included a section entitled "The Rise of the Legal Evidence Model" in their book *Faith Has Its Reasons: An Integrative Approach to Defending Christianity.*[21] Their designation of legal apologetic as a "model" suggests that it is something more than a genre, style, or rhetoric, but not a distinct "school." Further complicating the issue at hand is the question of which authors/works should be categorized as members of a legal apologetic school. For example, Philip Johnson's inventory of juridical apologetic authors includes the mathematician Gottfried Leibniz, a committed Christian who studied jurisprudence and contributed to the development of probability theory yet did not produce any work that could be classified as a legal apologetic.[22] Given the current ascent of legal elements within apologetics, this book will furnish a response to the question of whether the legal apologetic put forth by Montgomery and others comprises a distinct school, and, more broadly, it will provide a firmer grasp of what legal apologetics is. The purpose here is not to formulate a precise definition of legal apologetics. It is instead to move toward a substantially stronger understanding of its historical development, its distinctive characteristics, its relationships to other apologetical approaches, and its role in the defense and propagation of the faith in our society today.

The Strategy of this Book and its Sequence of Presentation

In addition to the analytical function of legal apologetics, this writer's interest in the topic gained impetus from Clifford's suggestion that a prospectively valuable study could "focus on an historical analysis of the development of the legal argument for the resurrection."[23] Therefore to achieve an understanding of legal apologetics, we will first trace the broad historical evolution of its development in the sections following.

Legal Apologetics in New Testament Times

As will be set forth in chapter 2, in this writer's view, the time period for this survey extends back nearly two thousand years, for "from the very beginning Christians have been called upon to defend their faith that Jesus is the Messiah, the Son of the Living God."[24] In his first full-length legal apologetic, Montgomery stated that "readers of older apologetic literature are aware that lawyers and legal scholars have been concerned with the credibility of Christianity for quite some time."[25] But there is substantial reason to maintain that the history of legal apologetics extends further back than the seventeenth century and Hugo Grotius. Indeed, the present writer will contend that the New Testament writers, notably Paul and, more particularly, Luke in both Acts and his own Gospel narrative, put forth evidential apologies for the resurrection that were designed to meet the legal standards of the period.

Legal Apologetics from the Patristic Period to the Enlightenment

After the New Testament period, from the time of Augustine to the Reformation, evidential apologetics virtually disappeared. However the Reformation and the following Enlightenment initiated theological and intellectual movements that encouraged both an empirical basis and a motivation for a radical departure from the apologetic paradigm of the patristic era and the Middle Ages. In response to the rise of Deism, strict empiricism, and modern scriptural criticism, the conceptual basis of a legal apologetic was bolstered in the eighteenth century by the evidentialism of Joseph Butler and William Paley. While some five decades elapsed between Paley's compilation of Christian evidences and Greenleaf's pivotal contribution to legal apologetics, the central conceptual underpinnings of a legal apologetic school were in place well before Greenleaf's work.

Summary of Chapters 2 through 5

Chapters 2 through 5, therefore, lead us to conclude that legal apologetics has a history that is coextensive with Christianity itself, that it is unified by a shared understanding of the relationship between faith and reason, and that it requires a fact-based defense that seeks a "probable" judgment, which falls short of absolute certainty but would lead to a conclusive verdict within a court of law.

Chapter 6 turns to an identification of the salient features or tendencies that characterize contemporary legal apologetics. In this regard, it has been pointed out that "what distinguishes juridical apologetics as a distinct school of thought is the use of legal analogies or metaphors that are applied in the defense of Scripture."[26] In the present writer's estimation, however, the legal apologetic model is characterized by more than "analogies," "metaphors," and other rhetorical devices. It lies within the "evidential family" of apologetics, yet it hinges upon concepts and procedures that are firmly established within and specific to Anglo-Saxon jurisprudence.

In chapter 7, we will first consider a comparative examination of the legal model, as a form of evidentialism and other apologetic models or "schools." As will be discussed at length in chapters 7 and 8, periodic efforts to develop a comprehensive classification of contemporary Christian apologetics have not generated a scholarly consensus about the validity or the explanatory power of any categorical design. There are, of course, some significant, clear-cut contrasts to be drawn among accepted apologetic approaches. This will be especially noted between the evidentialism championed by Montgomery, on the one hand, and the presuppositionalist apologetics espoused by Cornelius Van Til, on the other.[27] As Steven Cowan's collection of essays on apologetic "views" indicates, the field is not simply divided into evidentialist and presuppositionalist camps because we must also recognize "classic" and "cumulative case" apologetics, each of which adopts a model that departs from both the evidentialist and presuppositionalist points of view.[28] Of equal importance, within the evidential family, there are meaningful differences to be drawn between historical and legal apologetics. Indeed, while acknowledging substantial overlap, Clifford characterizes them as "distinct" schools.[29] The analysis presented in chapter 8 supports Clifford on this count; it finds that there are important points of variance between the historical and legal models.

In chapter 9, this book concludes with an assessment of how closely a "Montgomery-type" legal apologetic accords with the specific needs of the times in which we now live; that is, roughly from the mid-1960s to the present. As William Dyrness wrote in the early 1980s, "Today's emphasis on apologetics results more from historical and cultural factors than from religious or philosophical ones."[30] Although every "school" of contemporary apologetics has historical beginnings and can be distinguished from rival perspectives, it is also apparent that apologetics is a response to the predominant challenges that the central claims of Christianity faces, both outside and inside the Christian set of beliefs. As it now stands, the central miracle claim of Christianity, which is the resurrection and deity of Jesus, is subject to assault from various quarters. For example, in the nineteenth and early twentieth centuries, these assaults came from the residue of "higher criticism" in biblical scholarship, a subjectivist or personal orientation in Christian thought, and a corresponding tendency on the part of liberal theologians to deny factual status to the physical resurrection of Jesus. At the same time, modern Western civilization has become infused with secularism and a multicultural outlook in which all religious and nonreligious belief systems are accorded equal value. Finally, optimistic, anthropocentric humanism itself has been challenged by a postmodernist deconstructionism that is most apparent within academic circles but nonetheless exerts a pervasive and strong *skeptical influence* on the environment in which faith claims are advanced in the church. In the present writer's estimation, a legal apologetic focused squarely on proving the factual reality of Jesus' resurrection is particularly well suited to our times.

2

Development of Apologetics during the New Testament and Early Patristic Era

Introduction

Comprehensive scholarly accounts of the history of Christian apologetics are few in number, and existing works necessarily reflect the denominational affiliations and biases of their respective authors. The most widely referenced text in the field is Avery Dulles's book, *A History of Apologetics;* and while Dulles attempts to maintain a modicum of objectivity and balance, he is a Roman Catholic, and his survey tends to focus on apologetics written by Roman Catholic authors. In this connection it should be noted that few of these authors are members of the evidential "family" to which the legal apologetic definitely belongs. In the preface to the first edition of his book, Dulles noted a scarcity of studies on the history of apologetics and argued that the field was in a state of decline. He attributes this to a popular alienation from the stereotypical apologist as "aggressive, opportunistic persons who try, by fair means and foul, to argue people into joining the Church."[31] To some extent, any writer who approaches the task of unraveling the historical threads that have contributed to the development of a specific apologetical "school" must acknowledge that his or her own theological presuppositions will influence the selection of a past history and the explanation of its relationship to that school. Moreover, just as apologetics cannot be hermetically sealed off from theology, it is closely joined with evangelism and the mission or missions to which the historian believes apologetics should be harnessed. In what follows, the present writer can only touch upon a broad outline of the legal apologetic's development and, in doing so, recognizes that his own faith-based assumptions are bound to result in a particular slant.

Apologetics in the New Testament and Early Patristic Era

"Before being an apologetic, Christianity was of course a message," one that was driven by the Great Commission and the conviction of Jesus' followers in the truth of the resurrection.[32] From reading the Gospel narratives, we find "little resemblance to modern apologetical treatises" and little in the way of sustained argumentation.[33] Likewise, the conservative Protestant theologian Benjamin Warfield cautioned his readers that they "must not confuse the apologies of the early Christian ages with the modern formal study of apologetics."[34] However "while none of the New Testament writings is directly and professedly apologetic, nearly all of them contain reflections of the Church's efforts to exhibit the credibility of its message. This would include an answer to the obvious objections that would have arisen in the minds of its adversaries, prospective converts, and candid believers."[35] Therefore the New Testament describes situations in which the earliest Christians were compelled to stand before hostile tribunals, authorities, and forums to bear witness to their faith and the reasons or evidence for it.[36] Whether their primary aim was conversion or a simple plea for political tolerance, Jesus' disciples were effectively forced to engage in apologetical activity.

New Testament Apologetics

We probably all realize from our own studies of Scripture that not only did the Christians of the first century employ apologetics, but also that "the legal paradigm has its roots in the early church."[37] For example, in his first epistle, the apostle Peter told his fellow believers that they should always be "ready to make a defense [*apologia*] to everyone who asks you to give an account for the hope that is in you, yet with gentleness and reverence" (1 Pet. 3:15 NASB). In some modern versions of this text, the word "explanation" appears instead of "defense," but the original

Greek text uses *apologia*, which specifically denoted a type of verbal argument common to Greek (and Roman) courts such as the Athenian forum in which Socrates was purportedly tried and sentenced.[38] The central element of this apology in 1 Peter 3:15 was the conviction that Jesus of Nazareth physically died on the cross and underwent a resurrection into a physical body that was seen and touched by His immediate disciples and followers. In the first epistle to the Corinthians (15:14-17), Paul proclaimed that if Jesus did not rise from the dead, the Christian faith was without substance and the gospel that he proclaimed was meaningless. Also in that same epistle, Paul consistently expressed his distrust of Greek philosophy and stressed the superiority of revelation from God to human reason.[39]

The first Christians were, of course, primarily Jewish converts, and the standard against which claims for the resurrection were tested within the Jewish community was not that of evidence based on objective fact but the assertion that Jesus was the Messiah foretold by the prophets and psalmists centuries before.[40] One scholar has said, "The first Christians had no doubt that the life and ministry of Christ fulfilled the Old Testament. They felt that if something could not be proved from the Old Testament, it could not be proved at all."[41] To satisfy the demands of prophecy, the first Christian evangelists cited hard factual correspondences between the life of the Jewish Messiah and that of Jesus of Nazareth. Their apologetic, then, was *evidential* in thrust and rested in large part upon inferences that could be drawn from factual or empirical observations.

The Apologetics of the Apostle Paul

As a student of the school of the Pharisee Gamaliel in his pre-conversion life, St. Paul was deeply acquainted with the Jewish law and its reliance on precedents.[42] In his life as Saul, Paul was raised within the cosmopolitan port at Tarsus, where he was first exposed to Hellenic culture and became familiar with the pleadings that took place in Greek forums. Paul's method of defending the faith reflected a legalistic turn of mind and employed the procedures and the rhetoric of judicial proceedings.[43] Several scholars have argued that in Acts, Luke recorded Paul's apologetics with Greek and Roman tribunals as conforming closely to the formats of their respective legal systems.[44] Before the council at the Areopagus in Athens (Acts 17:16-20), for instance, Paul offered multiple forms of proof in support of Christian miracle claims, including the fulfillment of prophecy, the testimony of his fellow disciples, and his own, firsthand encounter with the risen Christ. He argued that Jesus was the "historically verifiable fulfillment of natural religion and the natural law tradition."[45] Paul's reliance upon multiple forms of proof was in accordance with the evidentiary standards of Greek courts,[46] and, "the only testimony Luke means to offer (in Acts) is that which would satisfy a court of law. This demands twofold or threefold testimony: this then is the significance of his repeated use of the principle of two foldness."[47] Also in his Roman apologetic (Acts 24-26), the apostle Paul "not only appeals to Roman rules of evidence (Acts 24:19-20) . . . his apologetic here is based on the Roman legal custom of four or five standard components with the defense answering specific accusations."[48]

Apologetics in the Gospel of Luke

In his Gospel account, Luke put forth a diligently researched, historical apologetic on behalf of the resurrection. According to William Lane Craig,

> In Luke-Acts . . . we have a sophisticated example of an early Christian argument for the resurrection. . . . the first systematic attempt to establish the resurrection through historical evidence; for with Luke's lengthy and close scrutiny of the facts, his research into eyewitness reports, his descriptions of unmistakable appearances of Jesus alive from the dead, and his repeated emphasis on the first-hand testimony of the apostolic preachers, a historical proof for the resurrection, among other things, is exactly what he is about.[49]

Although Luke did not intend his narrative to serve as a legal proof, he was intent upon organizing both direct and circumstantial evidence that Jesus died by crucifixion, that the tomb in which he was laid to rest by Joseph of Arimathea was found open and empty, and that eyewitnesses subsequently encountered the resurrected Jesus on the first Easter and for forty days thereafter.

Apologetics in the Gospel of John

Written decades after Luke, the Gospel of John was authored by an early Christian who claimed to have been one of the twelve apostles and a member of Jesus' "inner circle." Apparently John's Gospel follows a lawsuit model in its defense of the claim that Jesus rose from the dead.[50] John presents eyewitness testimony in support of the claim that the resurrection is a historical fact, describing events that he saw with his own eyes and a risen Christ that he touched with his own hands. Moreover, John proclaimed that this miraculous series of events proved that Jesus was not merely a man who somehow rose from the dead but that He was, in fact, the Son of God. Toward that end, the author drew upon the testimony of John the Baptist, the words and works of Christ, and the witness of the apostles and the Holy Spirit.[51]

To be sure, the reasons the New Testament writers used to protect their conviction that Jesus was resurrected by the Father and was one with Him extended well beyond objective fact. However, the core of the earliest apologetic arguments clearly included Christian evidences, and they were presented with the aim of satisfying standards of proof that were embodied within the law or legal systems of those with whom they conversed. Indeed, Jesus Himself told His adversaries that they would be given an unmistakable sign of His divinity, the "sign of Jonah," in the form of His death and His Resurrection after three days of entombment (Matt. 12:39-40). *Given all this, we must agree that the origins of the "legal apologetic" can be found within the New Testament itself.*

The Patristic Apologists

Justin Martyr

The first Christian works to assume the title of "apology" were two treatises written by Justin Martyr in the middle of the second century A.D. These were written for submission to the Roman authorities.[52] Neither of these works attempted to demonstrate the factuality of Jesus' resurrection. They were instead pleas for civil tolerance toward Christians and efforts to dispel unjust condemnations brought against them by Roman "patriots." Nevertheless, Justin did introduce a piece of circumstantial evidence in arguing that the current moral behavior and good citizenship of his Christian associates was grounded in their belief in the resurrection of Jesus. At an earlier date, Justin composed his work *Dialogue with Trypho the Jew.* His apologetic in this work focused on demonstrating that Jesus was the Messiah foretold in the Jewish prophetic literature. But there, as in his later apologies, Justin did not call upon eyewitness testimony for the risen Christ.

Origen

One of the first Christian apologetic works composed in response to a formal written attack on the Christian faith was Origen's *Contra Celsum*.[53] Under the title of *True Doctrine*, Celsus (a Platonist and polytheist) wrote that Christianity was inherently irrational in demanding faith without critical examination. He also claimed that Christians shunned public debate and that the resurrection of Jesus was either a pretense perpetrated on naïve believers or a mass delusion.[54] In his response, Origen first argued that critical investigation of Christian miracle claims was unnecessary and that no true believer could ever be shaken from his faith by flawed pagan argumentation. Nonetheless, expanding on Justin and anticipating Augustine, Origen presented post-hoc circumstantial evidence of Jesus' divinity. He wrote, "The evidence of Jesus' divinity are the Churches of the people who have been helped, the prophecies spoken about him, the cures which are done in his name, the knowledge and wisdom of Christ, and reason which is to be found in those who know how to advance beyond mere faith, and how to search out the meaning of the divine scriptures."[55] Oddly, Origen did not offer the testimony of eyewitnesses to Jesus' resurrection within the evidence that he used to refute Celsus.

Tertullian

The reader will note that none of the sources covered to this point was written by a member of the legal profession. It was in A.D. 197 that Tertullian became the first lawyer to put forth an apology for the Christian faith.[56] Tertullian was a skilled and successful legal advocate who appeared in Roman tribunals before and after his conversion to Christianity. Like Justin, Tertullian's objective was not to demonstrate the validity of Christian miracles, including the resurrection. His goal was to prove the value of Christianity by highlighting the good citizenship and high moral character of its adherents. Tertullian did not mention the resurrection, and, while he used legal rhetoric, his treatise did not assume the form of a court pleading. Like the presuppositionalists of our own age, Tertullian rejected the idea that pagans could be converted through an appeal to their reason. He maintained that belief in the claims of Christianity came solely through revelation. In his work titled *Prescription against Heretics*, Tertullian initially contemplated mounting a legal defense against Gnostics.[57] But he dismissed the project and explained that pagans should not be allowed to present their "petitions" to orthodox Christians. Apart from the author's vocation, the most relevant aspect of Tertullian's *Apology* for the development of a legal apologetic appears in a passage that reads: "What has Jerusalem to do with Athens, the Church with the Academy, and the Christian with the heretic? . . . I have no use for a Stoic or a Platonic or a dialectic Christianity. After Jesus Christ we have no need for speculation, after the Gospel no need of research."[58] Ironically, the first Christian lawyer apologist categorically rejected both the metaphysics of Greek philosophy *and* empirical evidence as a basis for defending the faith.

3

Development of Apologetics from Augustine to the Reformation

Biblical Faith and Philosophy (Synthesis)

Around A.D. 270, Porphyry, a student of Neoplatonic philosophy, wrote a tract under the title of *Against the Christians,* in which he attacked the authenticity of the New Testament, as well as the historicity of Jesus' ancestry, His miracles, and the resurrection.[59] This was just the first in a succession of Neoplatonic critiques of Christianity that persisted through the conversion of Constantine in the early fourth century. While the first church historian, Eusebius, formulated a rebuttal to *Against the Christians*, the principal response of the patristic era to the challenge launched by Neoplatonists was to appropriate materials from the Stoic and Platonic philosophers.[60] When the church fathers of the fourth century were confronted with the problem of the relationship between Christian doctrine and Platonism, "the leading apologists were almost unanimous in opting for a synthesis of Biblical faith with classical culture."[61] It was Augustine of Hippo who best exemplified this synthesis of philosophy with faith. By following this approach, Augustine established an environment that was not friendly to evidential apologetics of any kind.

Augustine (Separation of Noumenal and Phenomenal)

In the *Confessions of Augustine*, Augustine did offer a lowercase apology for the Christian faith grounded in his presentation of the church as a moral miracle. He wrote about three, interpenetrating "incredibilities": the resurrection itself, the fact that so many people believed in the resurrection, and the unlikelihood that men of simple, humble origin had persisted through persecution in holding a faith that had grown into the church of the fourth century.[62] Such evidential signs, however, were subordinate to Augustine's adoption of Plato's metaphysical idealism. Like Plato, Augustine held that the human mind has certain innate ideas, ideals, or "forms" that exist independently of sensory experience. More specifically, in Augustine's apologetic, human beings intuitively sense that they exist and they have a corresponding and innate sense that God exists.[63] Augustine, however, was not a "fideist," for he asserted that "in his soul man perceives the existence of God in the same way that he perceives his own existence; and because the two are in a mutual relationship, man perceives both to be true simultaneously."[64] It is through an instinctive ability, then, that human beings access the idea of God. It is by that same process that they know themselves to exist and, therefore, that God must exist just as human beings are known to exist. Through a totally opposed channel, then, Augustine arrived at much the same conclusion as Tertullian. Both of these "apologists" held that "nobody believes anything unless he is first convinced that it ought to be believed."[65] For the Roman lawyer Tertullian, belief comes from revelation; for the theologian Augustine, faith comes from a capacity that God has implanted in the human soul. John Warwick Montgomery would later point out *that Augustine's theology put forward a complete separation between the noumenal and the phenomenal worlds, which is directly contrary to the Scriptures' insistence that God became man, and that the infinite became finite.*[66]

Anselm (A Transition)

Augustine remained the preeminent theologian of the Church until the Scholastic period of the High Middle Ages. Between the fall of Rome and the Scholastic revival of the eleventh century, Christian apologetics was largely restricted to assaults upon Islam, Judaism, and heresies. The general level of learning in the West declined while the Catholic

Church exerted hegemony over political and cultural life throughout Europe.[67] It was in the second half of the eleventh century, that the British monk Anselm began a *transition* that would ultimately precipitate a new understanding of the relationship between faith and reason. As a transitional figure, Anselm has defied easy characterization. He has been alternatively referred to as a fideist and as a rationalist.[68] In his *Proslogion*, Anselm advanced an ontological argument for the existence of God. In essence, Anselm contended that the very fact that we can conceive of a perfect being, that is, of God, "proves" that He must exist.[69] As with Augustine, knowledge of God does not require any empirical data, and understanding is still conditional upon faith. Unlike Augustine, however, Anselm believed that faith is *objectively* rational. Human efforts to understand God are not limited to intuition, but extend to logical operations, and rational inquiry is a legitimate means for "knowing" God.[70] With Anselm, then, reason came substantially nearer to faith than it had been in the history of Christian thought since the early patristic age.

Thomas Aquinas (Moving toward Evidentialism)

It was not until Thomas Aquinas in the thirteenth century that a rationalist outlook took full command of Christian theology and apologetics. As had been the case in the late third century, this significant change was precipitated by an external threat. The Spanish Arab Averroes had put forth an Islamic interpretation of the Greek philosopher Aristotle that penetrated deeply into Christendom. In conjunction with the decline of the Platonic theology of Augustine and the failures of the Crusades, simple Christian triumphalism became increasingly untenable. Aquinas met the challenge by recapturing Aristotle's inductive approach to knowledge, including knowledge of God.[71] As Hoffecker summarized his use of Aristotle, St. Thomas

> sought to show the feasibility of a natural metaphysic, that is, a rational investigation of what lies beyond physical reality. Using the senses to analyze the physical world enables man to know something of the reality that transcends this realm. Reason equips the Christian and the non-Christian alike to (1) begin with the immediate data of sense experience, (2) reflect on that experience, and (3) come to a mutual conclusion that a God exists who transcends the physical reality known by the senses. Knowledge of God comes primarily through inferences drawn from the physical world rather than through personal experience felt in the heart.[72]

In his *Summa Contra Gentiles*, Aquinas asserted that empirical observations can serve as a basis for the formulation of generalizations or laws about the workings of the world around us, which, in their turn, can be used to demonstrate the existence of a higher realm in which God must, of necessity, exist.[73] On these grounds, Thomas set forth his famous "Five Ways" of demonstrating God's existence, each of which entails a cause-and-effect relationship and each of which denies the possibility of an infinite regression: God must exist (1) as the unmoved first mover; (2) as the uncaused first cause of all things; (3) as the necessary (noncontingent) being who anchors the existence of the contingent entities in nature; (4) as the perfect being that transcends everyday experiences of the good; and, (5) as the source of the order (intelligent design) that one finds throughout the natural realm.[74]

Aquinas's five proofs are still integral to what might be called the "classic, two-step" Christian apologetic approach. Aquinas did not contemplate the use of empirical inferences in support of finding the factuality of specific historical events. Consequently, his proofs offer virtually nothing to resurrection apologetics grounded in the witness of Scripture and/or circumstantial evidence.[75] But Aquinas reintroduced inductive argument into the defense of Christian belief, and in this sense his works have a remote connection to the evidentialist apologetic that would emerge with the recovery of the indispensable source of modern apologetic thought, the New Testament.

4

Development of Apologetics during the Reformation and the Enlightenment Periods

Apologetic Development during the Reformation

The Reformation was not accompanied by a spurt in apologetic activity. "None of the great reformers was deeply involved in the immediate problems of winning over non-Christians to the faith; hence, they had little to say about apologetics in the strict sense of the term."[76] Neither of the Reformation's principal theologians (Luther and Calvin) developed a distinctive apologetic,[77] and while Luther occasionally disagreed with the Jews, he was not interested in their conversion.[78] Moreover, the centerpiece of Luther's theology, justification through faith alone, was more compatible with Augustine's presuppositionalism than with the rationalism of Thomas's apologetic.

Luther's Contribution (The Bible as the Primary Source of Truth)

As John Warwick Montgomery has recently pointed out, during the first century of the Reformation, the emergence of a distinctive apologetic stance awaited the completion of a more urgent task, the development of a trustworthy Bible.[79] Luther harbored a profound distrust of Thomistic theology with its synthesis of Aristotelian philosophy with Christian faith, and he categorically rejected the pope's claimed authority to infallibly resolve differences in scriptural interpretation. He called for a return to basics through the reintroduction of the Bible as the primary source of Christian thought.[80] By doing so, he reoriented apologetics from a "top-down" process, originating in empirical generalizations from which inferences can be drawn, to a "bottom-up" process, moving from specific and concrete claims embodied in the New Testament, notably the assertion that the resurrection occurred, to broad proclamations about the nature of God.[81] Owing to Luther's rediscovery of the Gospels, "evidential apologetics turned out to be no less than *the epistemological handmaid of genuine Reformation theology*."[82] At bottom, the Reformation clearly favored a Scripture-based apologetic, and this necessarily brought with it an emphasis upon the authenticity of Scripture and the credibility of Jesus' disciples, including their firsthand experiences with the risen Christ.

Pre – Enlightenment Period

Hugo Grotius (The Truth of the Christian Religion)

The Arminian Calvinist Hugo Grotius is considered to be the first Protestant apologist, and with the publication of his treatise *The Truth of the Christian Religion*, Christian apologetics underwent a radical break from the metaphysical rationalism of the Middle Ages.[83] Originally composed in verse form in Grotius's native Dutch in 1627, an English language version of his apologetic first appeared in 1632. By that time, Grotius had amassed nearly three decades of experience as a lawyer and he had written the first text on international law. Several salient features of legal apologetics as it exists today, including its structure and its focus on the resurrection, can be traced back to this seminal work.[84]

The Truth of the Christian Religion was composed as the equivalent of a lawsuit addressed to Hieronymus Bignonius, who is identified in the text as "His Majesty's Solicitor in the Chief Court of Paris." It is composed of six brief books. In book 2, Grotius initiated his affirmative proof of the resurrection. He began with historical facts already in evidence, focusing on three data points that are acknowledged to be true by Christians and by non-Christian historians alike: (1) that a man named Jesus lived in Judea during the reign of the Emperor Tiberius; (2) that this Jesus died a shameful death; and, (3) that after His death, Jesus was worshipped by wise men. This yields a glaring inconsistency that demands explanation, for there is no logical reason why wise men should have worshipped an individual who died a shameful death. The only plausible explanation is that "upon diligent enquiry, such as becomes prudent for men to make in a matter of the highest concern to them, they found the reports which were spread abroad concerning His miracles were true."[85]

Having established a "minimal-facts" historical case for the miracle claims of the New Testament, Grotius proceeded to an explicitly legal argument for the resurrection, using eyewitness testimony of the risen Christ. He observed that this testimony was provided by multiple witnesses who claimed to have seen Jesus directly under a variety of circumstances. Consequently, it was unlikely that they all could have been deluded. Moreover, these individuals had no reason to lie about what they witnessed: "They could not hope for any honour from saying what was not true, because all the honours were in the power of the heathens, and Jews."[86] In fact, both the direct eyewitnesses to the resurrected Christ and those "wise men" who recorded and/or accepted their accounts were exposed to persecution as a consequence of their expressed beliefs. Taking these circumstantial considerations into account, Grotius concluded that the direct testimony of the witnesses must be credible.

By the early seventeenth century, the Bible itself had come under critical attack.[87] In book 3 of his treatise, Grotius addressed the historical reliability of the New Testament documents as a response to the two primary planks of the earliest source critics, namely, that the Gospels were written by untrustworthy authors and that they were marred by internal contradictions among the narrative.[88] Grotius replied that the Gospel narratives were written by the authors to whom they have been traditionally ascribed and that each of these men was well informed, honest, and therefore worthy of credence. He allowed that there are some inconsistencies among the Gospels but argued that these disparities are trivial when set alongside the overwhelming unity among them.[89] Although Grotius did not qualify the conclusion to his case as a "probability," he clearly weighed the facts at hand and found that the truth of Jesus' resurrection is firmly supported by the bulk of the available evidence.

Blaise Pascal (Proofs of Jesus Christ)

A concurrent recovery occurred among the Catholic apologists of the seventeenth century, but rather than returning to evidences from the Bible, they moved away from Thomistic rationalism and back toward Augustine's intuitive orientation. This contrary tendency can be discerned in the works of the French polymath Blaise Pascal. In his uncompleted (and thus fragmentary) *Thoughts,* or *Pensees*, Pascal included a section bearing the title "Proofs of Jesus Christ." Under this category, Pascal referred to the uniqueness of Jesus' teachings as an indirect demonstration of His divinity, pointing out, for example, that "Jesus said great things so simply that he seems not to have thought about them, and yet so clearly that it is obvious what he thought about them. Such clarity together with such simplicity is wonderful."[90] While Pascal accepted the core tenet that Jesus was fully divine and fully human, he observed that Catholic apologetics had failed to demonstrate either of these points, writing, "The Church has had as much difficulty in proving Jesus was man, against those who denied it, as in proving that he was God, and both were equally evident."[91] In Pascal's estimation, neither deductive nor inductive demonstrations of Jesus' divinity are valid; indeed, efforts to prove the core truths of Christianity are suspect on normative grounds. In fragment No. 298, Pascal declared: "The heart has its order; the mind has its own, which uses principles and demonstrations. The heart has a different one. We do not prove that we ought to be loved."[92] In a sense, Pascal transmutes Augustine's division of noumenal and phenomenal realms into cognitive and affective domains, paving the way for the existential subjectivity of Soren Kierkegaard in the early nineteenth century.

The Enlightenment

John Locke: (Empericism and Reason)

Running directly opposite to Pascal's return to intuition, the scientific revolution that accompanied the Reformation and the subsequent advent of Enlightenment philosophy in the seventeenth century established an environment in which empiricism ruled.

The foremost exponent of this paradigmatic shift was John Locke, who argued in his *Essay Concerning Human Understanding* that "revelation cannot be admitted against the evidence of Reason."[93] In both *The Reasonableness of Christianity as Delivered in the Scriptures* (1695) and his *Discourse on Miracles* (1703), Locke claimed that revelation and supernatural events could, in fact, be reconciled with human reason, and he assumed the factual validity of the miracles reported in the New Testament with their grounding in eyewitness observations.[94] Locke's epistemology did not reject the miracle claims of the Bible; it merely insisted that these claims be grounded in an interpretation of facts that accords with reason. As it turns out, however, Locke's principal disciple, David Hume, arrived at a radically different conclusion concerning the compatibility of supernatural events with inductive reasoning.[95]

The Age of Reason

The early eighteenth century witnessed a dramatic rise in "Christian evidences" as the basis of Protestant apologetics and was a crucial period for the evolution of the legal apologetic. Once again, the driving force behind these developments was a threat, or rather, a set of interrelated challenges to the revelations recorded in the Gospels.[96]

The Challenges of Deism

The most pervasive of these hostile forces was Deism. During what would later be characterized as the "Age of Reason," the Deists argued that the phenomenal or natural world operates according to its own laws, which can be discerned through the senses and constructed into an order through the application of man's rational faculties.[97] Therefore God's function in this worldview was relegated to setting the laws of nature into motion. From the Deists' standpoint, there was no logical reason for a deity to exist beyond this determining role and certainly no reason to believe that this lowercase god intervened in human affairs, to say nothing of assuming a human form.

The Challenges of Kant

Three further trends contributed to an environment in which evidential apologetics for the historical truth of Jesus' resurrection was virtually required. First, the last vestiges of St. Thomas's Scholastic proofs of God's existence were swept away by the German philosopher Immanuel Kant.[98] Kant argued for a strict dichotomy between absolute truth, on the one hand, and ordinary experience, on the other, asserting that generalizations derived from the latter could not be used to form inferences about "upper-level" truths such as God's existence. On the one hand, Kant's works on pure and practical reason run contrary to the essential assumption of the evidential/

legal apologetic that "facts" (including testimony) can be used to establish higher-order realities. In fact, the philosopher and literary critic G. E. Lessing applied Kant's views to religion and concluded that "the accidental truths of history can never become the proof of the necessary truths of reason."[99] On the other hand, however, Kant's assault on Thomism deeply undercut the basis of the "classical" apologetic, thereby clearing away deductive approaches to the truths of Christianity.

The Challenges of H.S. Reimarus

Between 1774 and 1777, Lessing published excerpts from Hermann Samuel Reimarus's *Apology for or Defense of the Rational Worshippers of God*, a Deist tract that utilized source criticism to highlight purported inconsistencies among New Testament accounts of the life, death, and resurrection of Jesus. The rhetoric and the evaluative standards of Reimarus's work were explicitly *legalistic*. He asked the rhetorical question, "How could anyone justify their religion and salvation upon the testimony of such varying witnesses?" And he concluded that the testimony embodied within the Gospels "would not be recognized in any secular court as valid and legal."[100] Reimarus's *Apology* may have been the first critical assault on biblical revelation to assume elements of a legal case.[101] Reimarus's skepticism about New Testament accounts of the resurrection, which called into question both the authenticity of the Gospel documents and the credibility of their contents, would be extended a century later by David Friedrich Strauss in *The Life of Jesus*. In effect, Reimarus issued the decisive work in what would become a prolonged "search" for the "historic" Jesus, a project that is still unfolding today. This quest rests upon the premise that the "real" Jesus was not the Son of God/Son of Man that He proclaimed Himself to be, but merely one son of a carpenter who lived and was crucified but did not rise from the dead. The appearance of "higher" biblical criticism in the eighteenth century focused on disproving the factuality of the resurrection. It also furnished additional impetus to evidential apologetics by using juridical standards for the admissibility of New Testament documents and the assessment of scriptural witness.

The Challenges of David Hume

While John Locke's empirical epistemology led him to conclude that the miracle claims of the Gospels are compatible with reason because they are factual, four decades later, Locke's disciple David Hume applied a far more stringent empiricism in his *Essay on Miracles* (1740). Hume argued that miracles are violations of the natural order, and while they may occur, their existence cannot be established through eyewitness testimony. In Hume's estimation, the occurrence of a reported miracle is so extraordinarily improbable that it is always more likely that the witness is either mistaken or untruthful.[102] Hume's principal "contribution" to evidential/legal apologetics lies in his assertion that extraordinary or astonishing events, such as the resurrection, demand a much greater weight of evidence than natural phenomenon.

Joseph Butler: (Foundational Apologetic Work)

A few years before Hume's essay appeared in print, Bishop Joseph Butler wrote what is undoubtedly the foundational work of evidential apologetics at large. This work is titled *The Analogy of Religion Natural and Revealed to the Constitution and Course of Nature*.[103] Like Hume, Butler embraced Locke's empirical epistemology: the human mind at birth is a blank slate, there are no innate ideas, and everything that we know comes to us through sensory experience. As Dulles characterized him, Butler was "a religious empiricist who has deeply reflected on the phenomena of nature and has assimilated the lessons of Locke's treatise on probability."[104] We shall return to the key topic of probability shortly, but for now we observe that Butler took square aim against the Deist contention that miracles are merely analogies. He argued that there are widely reported phenomena within the natural world that appear to be contrary to the laws of nature and, from a Deist perspective, are therefore irrational. Butler also declared, "He who believes that the God of Scripture is also the God of Nature should expect to find similar problems in both Scripture and Nature."[105] After showing that unexplainable and miraculous events do occur in nature, Butler turned to an affirmative argument for the New Testament. He placed the burden of proving the miracles to be false upon the shoulders of the skeptics. Butler wrote that "upon the whole: as there is a large historical evidence, both direct and circumstantial, of miracles wrought in attestation of Christianity, collected by those who have written on the subject; it lies upon unbelievers to show why this evidence is not to be credited."[106] The direct evidence for the resurrection that was cited by Butler encompassed eyewitness testimony, including Paul's encounter with the risen Christ. The circumstantial evidence presented by Butler included an empty-tomb argument and the failure of the skeptics to advance a stronger case for naturalistic explanations of it than the case for an actual miracle, as well as the subsequent growth of the Christian faith despite persecution.

As noted in passing immediately above, Butler acknowledged that inferences drawn from empirical "facts" cannot yield perfectly certain conclusions.[107] Following Locke, he realized that the human capacity to distinguish between truth and fiction is necessarily imperfect. This does not render the task of trying to discriminate between them meaningless, because, as Butler put it, "probability is the very guide of life."[108] In fact, almost all of human decisions, including those that have the gravest consequences (such as a jury verdict in a capital case) rest "upon evidence of a like kind and degree of the evidence of religion."[109] In Montgomery's estimation, "Butler showed great wisdom in recognizing that probability is inherent in the empirical approach."[110] Any evidential apologetic for the "facts" embodied in Scripture must of necessity generate a probable, as opposed to a completely certain, finding. While Grotius allowed the existence of inconsistency within Gospel accounts, he did not acknowledge that his conclusion about the "truth" of the Christian religion was in any way limited to a probability. By introducing probability into the apologist's realm, Butler broke completely with the traditional standards of Christian apologetics.[111] Moreover, Butler declared that the individual Christian is under an affirmative obligation to determine the probability of the New Testament's assertions about Jesus. In this context he wrote that all men are obliged to "search the Scriptures in order to determine whether these claims (that Christ is man's divine savior) are credible."[112] Butler therefore served as an advocate for the defense of Jesus and His resurrection, but he left the task of reaching a judgment to the individual Christian.

Butler did, in fact, study both law and divinity at Oxford, and he held a doctorate in common law from that university. His *Analogy* is replete with legal terminology, with phrases such as "direct and circumstantial evidence." But unlike Grotius, he did not frame his apologetic as a legal argument *per se*.

Thomas Sherlock: (Response to Deism)

A contemporary of Butler's, Thomas Sherlock did use a juridical model in his *The Trial of the Witnesses of the Resurrection of Jesus*.[113] Sherlock was not a lawyer by trade, but prior to his elevation to the post of Bishop of London, he had served as a pastor to members of the legal profession in the city. Sherlock composed his legal apologetic as a response to the Cambridge Deist Thomas Woolston's *Discourse on the Miracles of Our Savior, in View of the Present Contest between Infidels and Apostates*. In that work, Woolston charged the witnesses to the risen Christ with perjury and asserted that the Gospel narratives are fraudulent. Sherlock replied that the witnesses were simple, honest men who had no reason to lie and whose religion required them to be truthful in their dealings. As to Woolston's point that the witnesses may have been deceived, Sherlock stated that under normal circumstances, people of ordinary intelligence can discriminate between a live man and a dead man. "So that a Resurrection considered only as a Fact to be proved by Evidence, is a plain Case: it requires no greater Ability in the Witnesses, than they be able to distinguish between a Man dead, and a Man alive: A Point, in which I believe every one living thinks himself a judge."[114] The eyewitnesses to the risen Christ, Sherlock concluded, were sane and forthright, and that, in his view, was enough to void Woolston's charges against them. Sherlock's *Trial* was extremely popular with London's citizens who were familiar with both common law procedures and the Bible's injunction against false testimony. Its publication evoked a series of six skeptical treatises from the Deist Peter Annent, to which Sherlock replied nearly twenty years after the submission of his first moot under the title of *The Sequel of the Trial of the Witnesses of the Resurrection of Jesus Christ*.[115] It is essential to note, however, that Sherlock did not attempt to prove the positive case for the resurrection but only to answer a set of narrow criticisms against some portions of the evidence for it.

William Paley: (The Importance of Evidence in Christian Apologetics)

By the end of the eighteenth century, the historical apologetic for the New Testament had reached a stage at which a summary of the available evidences was warranted. William Paley performed that consolidating function in his *A View of the Evidences of Christianity*. More of a compiler than an original apologist, Paley was a committed empiricist, who declared that "the truth of Christianity depends on leading facts and them alone."[116] Even more than Butler, Paley insisted that evidence must be evaluated from the standpoint of an "impartial" observer; in his work, presuppositions are entirely banished from the field.

In part 1 of *A View*, Paley first compared the attestation of pagan miracles, including mythical resurrection stories, to testimony for the miracles described in the New Testament. The former, Paley noted, typically involved only a single purported eyewitness (or none at all); the New Testament miracles, however, were substantiated by multiple sources, and they described events that took place in public that were seen by dozens of observers. These were bound to raise objections from those at the scene if they were in any way false. Since no objections were recorded, Paley concluded that the Gospel stories about Jesus are established "by more and more strong proofs than belong to almost any other ancient book what-ever."[117] As for charges of inconsistencies among the Gospel narratives, echoing Grotius's position, Paley dismissed them as insignificant, arguing that these four works are in substantial agreement with each other. With reference to the credibility of the eyewit-nesses to the risen Christ, Paley insisted that the apos-tles were simple, honest men who taught the virtue of honesty and that the earliest Christians spread the good news of Jesus' resurrection despite the suffering and hardship that they were compelled to undergo. Like Butler, Paley insisted that "Christian evidences" did not (and could not) prove the "hard fact" of any event (miraculous or ordinary), and he stressed that no one actually saw Jesus' arise from death and exit the tomb. Nevertheless, the accumulated direct and circumstantial evidence enabled Paley (and his readers) to arrive at the conclusion that it was more probable that the resurrection occurred than that any alternative explanations (that the witnesses lied or were deluded, that the apostles constructed a myth, and the like) were true. In part 2 of his book, Paley brought the evidence into the present day, arguing that it is extremely difficult to account for the Easter faith without accepting the resurrection and that the beliefs about the resurrection reported in the New Testament were virtually identical to those held by contemporary believers in late eighteenth-century England.

Johnson's essay on juridical apologists includes a reference to Paley, but, unlike Butler, Paley was not an attorney. Still, he reportedly pursued a lifelong interest in the law, he served as a justice of the peace, and the influence of the law on Paley's apologetic "has been underplayed."[118] There is no doubt that Paley construed his role as that of a historian who employed broad principles of common law in making the case for the credibility of the New Testament at large and the resurrection in particular. In Craig's view, Paley's synthesis of Christian evidences represents the "the high water mark of the historical apologetic."[119] By the time that Paley wrote, all the elements of a "general" legal apologetic for the resurrection were firmly in place. The emergence of a "technical" legal apologetic, however, did not occur until midway through the nineteenth century with the work of Simon Greenleaf.

5

Development of Apologetics in the Nineteenth and Early Twentieth Centuries

Soren Kierkegaard and the Impact of Subjective Thinking

During the nineteenth century, Pascal's "reasons-of-the-heart" rejection of rational apologetics was replicated within Protestant circles by the first full-fledged existentialist philosopher, Soren Kierkegaard; and with Kierkegaard subjectivism began to influence Protestant theology. At the same time, Strauss and the higher critical school of Bible studies intensified the effort to discover a Jesus apart from Scripture, a "historic" Jesus shorn of all divinity.[120] Although historical apologetics began to decline under the heavy weight of existential philosophy, the legal apologetic actually enjoyed ascension, due chiefly to Greenleaf's *Testimony of the Evangelists.*

At the start of the nineteenth century, Soren Kierkegaard introduced a radically subjective interpretation of Christian faith as a personal, quasi-mystical experience that was immediate and not amenable to rational explanation.[121] According to Gary Habermas, Kierkegaard believed that the resurrection was an actual, literal event, but nevertheless he maintained that it could not be approached through empirical methods or any rational activity.[122] Surveying all of Kierkegaard's religious writings, Dulles found that "in many passages Kierkegaard seemed to reject the entire apologetical effort as illegitimate."[123] In his *On Authority and Revelation*, Kierkegaard stated that if efforts to make Christianity "plausible" had succeeded, this "would have lost everything and entirely quashed Christianity."[124] Since the time of Anselm and certainly after Grotius, Christian apologetics had pointed outward toward inferences from empirical data. Starting with Pascal, and much more insistently in Kierkegaard, proof of the reality of biblical revelation reverted to an inward perspective in which individual ineffable experience, rather than a consensual reality, was paramount.[125]

Even as this intellectual current was unleashed within European intellectual and religious life, "higher" source criticism continued its assault on both the textual authenticity and the content validity of the Gospels. In 1846, David Friedrich Strauss published *The Life of Jesus.*[126] Building on Reimarus, newly discovered textual materials, and archaeological findings, the bulk of Strauss's work was dedicated to dispelling the "myths" of the Gospels.[127] Its publication provoked intense debate between unbelievers and committed Christians in Europe, and a correlative tendency among the latter to retreat into fideism and/or the private realm of existential Christian belief.

Simon Greenleaf and the Advancement of Legal Apologetics

At the same time, however, the American legal scholar Simon Greenleaf became "*the* pivotal figure in juridical apologetics."[128] When he wrote his principal apologetic work in 1846, Greenleaf had published the first volume of *A Treatise of the Law of Evidence,* a work that would become the "standard authoritative text in nineteenth-century American jurisprudence."[129] Holding the chair as the Royall Professor of Law at Harvard University, Greenleaf was already recognized as the foremost American authority on common law evidence in the nineteenth century.[130] He applied this knowledge and experience to countering the critique of the Gospels that had been rendered by Strauss and his precursors.

In 1846, Greenleaf published *An Examination of the Testimony of the Four Evangelists by the Rules of Evidence Administered in Courts of Justice, with an Account of the Trial of Jesus*, a text that has been reprinted many times since then and is now generally referred to as *Testimony of the Evangelists.*[131] Akin to Paley, Greenleaf avoided bringing presuppositions to the task of assessing the credibility of the Gospels. Early in this work Greenleaf informed his readers that "in examining the evidences of the Christian religion it is essential to the discovery of the truth that we bring to the investigation, a mind freed, as far as possible, from existing prejudice and open to conviction."[132] Like Butler and Paley, he emphasized that the Gospels were composed by their respective authors as actual, factual accounts. "The foundation of our religion is a basis of fact," Greenleaf declared, "the fact of the birth, ministry, miracles, death, resurrection and ascension of Jesus are true. These are related by the Evangelists as having actually occurred, within their personal knowledge. Our religion, then, rests on the credit due to these witnesses."[133]

Rules of Evidence

The most significant aspect of Greenleaf's *Testimony* was the author's imposition of juridical "rules of evidence" upon the assembled data. The first of these tests was the "ancient document rule" for determining whether an "old" manuscript should be admitted into legal proceedings. According to Greenleaf, the ancient document rule stipulates that "every document, apparently ancient, coming from the proper repository or custody, and bearing on its face no evident marks of forgery, the law presumes to be genuine, and transfers to the opposing party the burden of providing it to be otherwise."[134] As will be brought forth in chapter 6, in both Greenleaf's and Montgomery's analysis of the Gospels, these works satisfy the ancient document test. The second rule concerned the superiority of direct eyewitness testimony over mere hearsay, because, "in matters of public and general interest, all persons must be presumed to be conversant, on the principle that individuals are presumed to be conversant with their own affairs."[135] Not only does the burden of proving a suit brought against a defendant rest with the prosecution, as a third rule for assessing evidence Greenleaf declared that "in trials of fact by oral testimony, the proper inquiry is not whether it is possible that the testimony may be false, but whether there is sufficient probability that it is true."[136]

The Fivefold Rule and "Technical" Legal Apologetic

As the means for evaluating the contents of testimony furnished by eyewitnesses, Greenleaf constructed a fivefold rule from his experience as a jurist. "The credit due to the testimony of witnesses depends upon, firstly, their honesty; secondly, their ability; thirdly, their number and the consistency of their testimony; fourthly, the conformity of their testimony with experience; and fifthly, the coincidence of their testimony with collateral circumstances."[137] Lastly, resonating with Sherlock's argument and responsive to Hume, Greenleaf acknowledged that the resurrection was an "astonishing" event that required a particular type of evidence, that is, evidence that is so plain and simple that it could be "easily seen and fully comprehended by persons of common capacity and observation."[138] Owing chiefly to his use of common-law criteria for determining the admissibility and value of Christian evidences, Greenleaf was identified by Clifford as the seminal writer within the subdiscipline of "technical" legal apologetics.[139] As Clifford would further observe, "This technical legal apologetic will strongly influence the American legal apologetic, whilst the English tradition follows a more general legal reasoning format."[140] Ultimately, the best known of the American legal apologetes, including Montgomery, can be best classified as belonging to the "technical" category since all of them utilize the rules and tests that Greenleaf identified in the mid-nineteenth century.

John Henry Newman and the Emphasis on the Convergence of Evidence

The last great Christian apologist of the nineteenth century was John Henry Newman, an Anglican clergyman who converted to Catholicism. Newman was familiar with Butler's *Analogy* and shared his views on the need to recognize that inferences drawn from historical evidence necessarily yield probable findings.[141] Newman drew a sharp distinction between Butler and Paley, expressing his admiration for the former while rejecting Paley's claim to neutrality in matters of faith, which he considered to be contrary to doctrine if not heretical.[142] In his "Essay on Miracles," Newman concluded that there is a "convergence of independent probabilities" that supports the factuality of the New Testament's miracle claims.[143] According to Montgomery, Newman employed a juridical standard in his emphasis upon convergences of evidence: "In court, although the witnesses of each individual witness don't match word for word, yet, since there's a convergence on the particular event in question, the jury is justified in acquitting or condemning a person on the weight of the testimony."[144] In some ways, Newman was closer to the "cumulative case" apologetic school than he was to evidential apologists. By any measure, he was not a member of the legal apologetic school. Nevertheless, his acceptance of "probability" within Christian apologetics is noteworthy insofar as it suggests the emergence of a common objective among Protestant and Catholic defenders of the faith: holding back the inroads of secular modernism upon orthodox beliefs.

Benjamin B. Warfield and the Need for Objectivity in Theology

Spurred by Greenleaf's work, evidential apologetics predominated in both Britain and the United States during the last quarter of the nineteenth century and the first two decades of the twentieth.[145] At the turn of the century, the conservative Protestant apologist Benjamin B. Warfield argued for establishing the truth of the New Testament by as direct a means as possible.[146] Taking an uncompromising evidentialist stance, Warfield proclaimed that "so soon as it is agreed that theology is a scientific discipline and has as its subject matter the knowledge of God, we must recognize that it must begin by establishing the reality as objective facts of the data upon which it is based."[147] The primary challenge to the credibility of the Gospels originated among a new generation of German source critics who continued to challenge their authenticity and their credibility.[148] Evidential apologetics was eminently suited to counteracting this assault from radical academics.[149]

Growth of Legal Apologetics in the Nineteenth and Early Twentieth Centuries

Under the circumstances mentioned above, it is not surprising that legal apologetics flourished, with a growing legion of lawyer-apologists publishing works that borrowed heavily from Greenleaf's tests and Paley's compilation of Christian evidences.[150] But by 1930, legal apologetics and, indeed, all forms of apologetics for the resurrection were suffering a general decline. There was a kernel of truth to the title of Willard Sperry's 1931 critique, *"Yes, But—." The Bankruptcy of Apologetics.*[151]

The General Decline of Apologetics in the Twentieth Century

In Dulles's estimation, the primary cause for the decline of apologetics between 1920 and 1950 was theological modernism as expounded, *more or less*, by Karl Barth.[152] Incorporating elements of Kierkegaard's existential thinking, Barth attacked traditional Christian belief in *Church Dogamtics.*[153] He argued that the factuality of Scripture was irrelevant; what counted for Christian believers was a direct "encounter" with God. Concurrently, Rudolph Bultmann dismissed evidence for the literal resurrection of Jesus, claiming that what Jesus experienced after His death belongs on a higher or "meta-historical" plane that is separate from the everyday world of historical phenomena.[154] In *Theology of the New Testament*[155] and *Kerygma and Myth: A Theological Debate*,[156] Bultmann declared that God's action in Jesus is "not a fact of past history open to historical verification."[157] Paradoxically, while he expressed personal belief in the resurrection, Bultmann aimed his efforts at "demythologizing" the Gospel narratives. Clearly, Barth and Bultmann's "modernity" are diametrically opposed to evidential apologetics of both the historical and the legal "schools."

The depressive impact of liberal theology on evidential apologetics persisted through the 1940s, even as historical and legal approaches to the resurrection continued to dominate the field. In 1948, for example, Edward John Carnell's standard textbook, *Introduction to Christian Apologetics*,[158] emphasized the need for empirically grounded defenses of the faith while acknowledging that such arguments for the miracle claims of Christianity (most notably the resurrection of Jesus) could only yield probable findings. He also maintained that the strength of such arguments can be bolstered by demonstrating the superior moral effects of belief in the lives of contemporary Christians. As Montgomery would later point out, in Carnell's view, although dialogue between Christians and non-Christians may lead to agreement about the historical facts of the resurrection, at bottom, the participants cannot come to a genuine consensus on the meaning of those facts because their interpretive frameworks are at insurmountable variance with each other.[159] Carnell's stance toward apologetics embodied both an evidential core *and* elements of the presuppositional model advanced by Cornelius Van Til.[160] Van Til's views and the presuppositional approach to apologetics will be discussed at greater length in chapter 8. At this stage, it is useful to note that while a strong scholarly consensus about the prospective utility of and need for an evidential apologetic has been in place for more than two hundred years, by the middle of the twentieth century, doubts had been raised about the scope of its usefulness as an argumentative strategy.

Writing in the early 1970s, Dulles was generally pessimistic about the outlook for apologetics. He nevertheless observed, "Since the 1950s, particularly among the younger Protestant theologians, there have been some indications that apologetics may be experiencing a revival."[161] In this context, Dulles cited the Lutheran theologian Paul Althaus's reply to Bultmann. While allowing that historical apologetics are not sufficient to occasion the conversion of some non-Christians, Althaus stated that they are nonetheless essential.

> The revelatory character of the history of Jesus is not known by means of historical reflection or historical reasoning. But on the other hand it is not known *without these*. For the gospel

deals with facts which, it is claimed, happened in this history of ours; it has 'historical facts' as its content, and its foundation in history is a part of its credibility.[162]

In 1964, John Warwick Montgomery published his highly influential *History and Christianity,* and a decade later he reinvigorated legal apologetics with *The Law above the Law.* But even before Montgomery's contribution to its articulation occurred, an explicitly juridical apologetic had been evolving for more than three centuries, and with Greenleaf's work it had acquired key and distinctive features. In the next chapter, the salient characteristics of contemporary legal apologetics will be identified, while in chapter 8, the distinctiveness of legal apologetics for the resurrection and the extent to which it differs from other apologetic approaches, will be taken into account.

6

The Characteristics of Contemporary Legal Apologetics

Introduction

Given the predominance of evidential approaches in the formal defense of the resurrection, the legal paradigm exemplified in Montgomery's work shares certain features with other apologetical "schools" that are currently active. The purpose of this chapter is simply to establish the characteristics of juridical apologetics. While some of these features are unique to it, in other instances the distinctiveness of the legal approach is basically a matter of degree or tendency.

Concentration upon the Resurrection of Jesus

Virtually all recently published legal apologetic studies have been devoted exclusively or primarily to setting forth the case for the resurrection. This is understandable given the paramount significance of the Easter event for Christianity. On the one hand, as Gary Habermas has put it, "There is widespread agreement among scholars today across a broad theological spectrum that the resurrection of Jesus is the central claim of Christianity."[163] At the same time, even though the resurrection itself was not seen, the Gospel narratives furnish an extremely rich body of purportedly factual information about the death of Jesus on the cross, His entombment, and His post resurrection appearances to the apostles and to large groups of His followers.[164] In essence, we have more, detailed, information concerning Jesus' resurrection than we have for any other single sequence of events recorded in the New Testament and, in fact, for any nonmiraculous occurrence in ancient history. Not only did Jesus foretell His own resurrection, but there are also several references to the life and the death of a future Messiah embodied within the Old Testament's prophetic books. Apologists following a legal model have analyzed and defended other topical domains, the "non-resurrection miracles of Jesus," for example. Nevertheless, the leading exponents of the legal apologetic have concentrated their efforts on the resurrection, and the defense of the resurrection's facticity is "the primary legal apologetic."[165]

Contrary to the contentions of Barth and Bultmann, the legal apologetic insists that the resurrection was literal and corporeal, that what the post hoc eyewitnesses encountered was not an effigy or the metaphysical spirit of Jesus but actual flesh and blood. Not only did the witnesses to the risen Christ see Jesus as He was before the crucifixion, but they also physically touched His body (notably the spear wound), and they observed Him as He performed miracles involving physical phenomena. As Montgomery observed, the corporeality of the risen Christ is grounded in the incarnation. All the Gospel writers, and most notably John, insist that in Jesus the Word became flesh, and from an orthodox perspective "at that point the sacred and the secular are united and no artificial barrier can be erected between them."[166] The objective of legal apologetics is *not* to show that some type of revival or reincarnation took place but that a fully human (and fully divine) Jesus rose from an otherwise ordinary human death.

A One-Step Approach

From Augustine onward, many efforts to establish the credibility of the resurrection event followed a two-step sequence. In essence, the "classical" model first proves the existence of God through intuitive or, more often, a rational procedure grounded in generalizations derived from inferences about the natural world, typically an argument that replicates or closely resembles one or more of Aquinas's

"Five Ways." Only after they have completed the argument for God's existence do practitioners of the classical approach initiate a historical/legal proof of the divinity of Jesus and/or the moral superiority of a Christian belief system that has the resurrection as its focal claim. Like evidential apologetics as a whole, the legal model employs a "one-step" methodology.[167] A key premise of the legal apologetic is that if Jesus did in fact rise from the dead, God the Father must exist.

The Objections of Robert Cavin to Legal Apologetics

Robert Cavin, one of the foremost critics of the legal apologetic, has commented that the "legal apologetic traditionally closes with the empty tomb and offers little or no evidence of the facts for eternal restoration."[168] By this, Cavin did not mean to suggest that the legal argument for the resurrection ends with an empty tomb; all practitioners of legal apologetics utilize eyewitness testimony to the risen Christ. What Cavin has argued is that Jesus may have lived, died, and lived again, but this does not necessarily demonstrate that He was divine and would live throughout eternity. Indeed, the Gospels record that Jesus performed the miracle of raising Lazarus from the dead, and yet Lazarus was not divine and he presumably died at the end of his natural, mortal life span.

Replies to Cavin

Legal apologists have dismissed Cavin's objections. Several have pointed out that Jesus did not merely live anew; His corpse was sealed in a tomb that an ordinary man (Lazarus for example) could not have escaped and that was guarded by Roman soldiers. According to Chrispin, then, "The resurrection suffices . . . the sealed tomb could not be conquered by a mere prophet, a simple or sincere religious leader, a well meaning martyr, or even a super angel. Only the One Who is both perfect Man and perfect God, as Jesus claimed to be, could rise from the dead in His resurrected body."[169] But the primary reply here is not that Jesus overcame barriers other than death itself. It is that Jesus said that He would do this and that His capacity to perform this miracle was predicated upon His being one with the Father. As Habermas and Licona have stated in *The Case for the Resurrection of Jesus*, Jesus' post resurrection appearances lend overwhelming support to His divinity claims.[170] Jesus' own understanding of "who" He was after the resurrection clearly indicates His conviction that His risen self was not an anomaly within the natural world but a transcendence necessitated by His integral part in the Trinity.[171] Montgomery's response to Cavin's point included the assertion that eternal resurrection is demonstrated by what Jesus said about Himself; and he added that because transcending physical mortality is the most fundamental felt need among all mankind, "then not to worship one who gives the gift of eternal life is hopelessly to misread what the gift tells you about the giver."[172] Jesus is unique among all the founders of the world's major religions; no other figure claimed to be divine. Nor do any other faiths assert that their founders (or any of their adherents, for that matter) came back from the dead. Thus, from Montgomery's perspective, "Jesus' deity in itself establishes the truth of the Christian message, over against competing religions and secular world-views."[173]

The Truth of Scripture

Lastly, Jesus' resurrection affirms the trustworthiness of the Bible at large and the Gospels in particular.[174] If it can be proved that Jesus rose from the dead and, in turn, that He was who He claimed to be, that is, the Son of God, then His message about the kingdom of God must be true, unless we are willing to entertain the outlandish notion that God is a liar. Jesus' resurrection confirms the message that He brought into the world, including the crucial proclamation that all human beings have hope for resurrection and eternal life (or for eternal damnation).[175] Given what Jesus' resurrection suggests, legal apologists are united in rejecting the need for any preliminary proof of God's existence.

Rules, Tests, and Criteria

Any empirical study that tests a formal hypothesis requires the establishment of protocols for determining which data can be included in the final analysis and what weight inferences drawn from that data should be accorded in the support or the refutation of that hypothesis. Whether they spell out (or even mention) these rules, tests, and criteria or not, all evidential apologists necessarily use them. In legal apologetics, these devices are generally drawn from common law standards for the submission of evidence, its assessment, and the standard of quantum of proof needed to reach a judgment.[176]

The Ancient Documents Rule

As noted in passing above, as the seminal scholar of a technical legal apologetic, Simon Greenleaf delineated a set of rules drawn from standard court-room practice as developed through the common law. In *The Law above the Law*, Montgomery presented a slightly modified version of the "ancient document rule" that embodies the same core concepts that appeared in Greenleaf's presentation of it, i.e., that the documents are "fair on their face" (indicating no tampering has taken place) and that they have been held in "reasonable custody" (suggesting that the documents at hand are facsimiles of the original texts).[177] In the case of the Gospels and Acts, the documentary material for a legal defense of the resurrection meets these tandem standards for *admissibility*. Granted, a period of several decades elapsed between the historical time of Jesus' crucifixion (presumably around A.D. 33, although possibly a few years earlier) and the composition of the first Gospel text (presumably Mark, written shortly before the destruction of the second temple). Nevertheless, this was a fairly short temporal interval, and we also have references to the resurrection in Paul's earliest letters (probably written about A.D. 48). The gap between the Easter event and its recording in the New Testament is brief, and the earliest manuscripts of the Gospels available to us accord closely with Scripture as we have it today.

Parol Evidence

The admissibility of the New Testament documents does not directly establish their credibility as factual accounts. While Greenleaf's treatise of 1846 did not contain reference to the "parol evidence" rule, Montgomery inserted this test into proceedings. The rule states that "external, oral testimony or tradition will not be received in evidence to add to, subtract from, vary, or contradict an executed written instrument such as a will."[178] According to Montgomery, its application to the legal apologetic for the resurrection means that all documents submitted to the "court" that expressly claim to be "executed and complete" must be taken at face value; that is, no extra documentary data can be introduced to twist the interpretation, such as a claim that the manuscript was actually an incomplete version of its author's intended message. In the case of the New Testament materials, the documents should be judged as "executed and complete."

The Hearsay Rule

As with Greenleaf, Montgomery asserted that in assessing evidence, eyewitness testimony is inherently stronger than hearsay. In Montgomery's legal apologetic, the "hearsay rule" means that "a witness must testify 'of his own knowledge,'" not on the basis of what he has heard indirectly from others.[179] In the case of the resurrection accounts that appear in the Gospels, the testimony comes from individuals, namely, the apostles, who said that they saw Jesus with their own eyes, heard Him speak with their own ears, and touched Him with their own hands. Their testimony amounts to primary source documentation.

Cross-examination

Montgomery's 1975 legal apologetic did not include Greenleaf's assertion that eyewitnesses be granted the "benefit of the doubt." Instead, Montgomery introduced the concept of cross-examination as a secondary means for assessing the credibility of witness testimony. Of course, legal apologetic proceedings do not furnish an opportunity for cross-examination. Yet as Montgomery has argued, "Applied to the apostolic proclamation, this rule underscores the reliability of testimony to Christ's resurrection which was presented contemporaneously in the synagogue—in the very teeth of opposition, among hostile cross-examiners who would certainly have destroyed the case for Christianity had the facts been otherwise."[180] Not only did the witnesses to the resurrection convey their experience to hostile parties, notably to Jews, but these hostile parties also had access to the very grounds on which Jesus was said to have appeared after the resurrection. Presumably, if they had evidence that countered the assertions of the eyewitnesses to Jesus' resurrection, these adversaries would have registered them at (or around) the time of Jesus' post crucifixion appearances. But we have no evidence that they did anything of the kind.

As Clifford has pointed out, "A major contribution of the legal apologetic is the criterion developed to test the competency and truthfulness of the witnesses to Christ's resurrection."[181] Montgomery and contemporary legal apologists have relied heavily upon Greenleaf's fivefold test to determine the probable veracity of eyewitnesses taken individually and collectively (see chapter 2).[182] In some instances, Montgomery and modern legal apologists seem to have added a sixth test, i.e., that testimony from "hostile" witnesses should be accorded greater weight, but this can be inferred from the third and fourth elements of Greenleaf's original measures of witness credibility.

Prototypical Structure

The presentational structure followed by the legal apologetes in making the case for the resurrection of Jesus varies. Indeed, as Clifford has observed, the case that Montgomery presented in *Human Rights and Human Dignity* exhibits some differences from the "Jury Returns" brief that Montgomery later presented as an essay in *Christians in the Public Square.*[183] Recognizing modest differences among legal apologists and even differences in the presentations of a single apologist over time, we can nonetheless discern a "prototypical" structure from a synthesis of Montgomery's works.

The structure of a representative legal apologetic for the resurrection embodies three broad components. Each of these components is based on empirical data, and while such evidence may be direct or circumstantial, no preliminary proofs of God's existence are "permitted" into the courtroom. The entire argument is based on inductive reasoning grounded in inferences drawn from specific pieces of evidence, direct and circumstantial.[184] Summarizing the elements of proof that must be met, Clifford has stated, "The main question is whether the pleaded inferential evidence for the resurrection is admissible, credible, relevant (material and probative value) and leads to a verdict."[185]

Testing Scripture against the Ancient Documents and Parol Evidence Rules

Because the direct evidence in the legal apologetic appears in New Testament documents, the first step in making the case for the factuality of the resurrection involves testing their admissibility against the "ancient document rule" and then applying the "parol evidence rule" to determine the admissibility of extra documentary evidence. In *Human Rights and Human Dignity*, Montgomery found that the Gospel narratives and the Acts of the Apostles meet the ancient document standard and are, therefore, admissible. He also determined that they satisfy the parol evidence rule and, as a consequence, extra textual evidence that calls their authenticity into question is *not* admissible.[186]

Greenleaf's Fivefold Criteria

The second step in a legal apologetic for the resurrection involves assessing the credibility of the contents of the documents that have been entered into the case, most crucially the direct testimony of Jesus' disciples. Applying Greenleaf's fivefold criteria, the prototypical legal apology would argue that the Gospel witnesses are honest, capable, and consistent with each other. Moreover, they had no motive to lie (and, in fact, strong reasons to avoid testifying, given the persecution of Christians by Jewish and Roman authorities), and their actions thereafter—the celebration of Easter and of Sundays for instance—were entirely consistent with having witnessed an extraordinary event on the first Easter Sunday. This component of the proof includes the key piece of circumstantial evidence in the legal case for the resurrection: the empty tomb. In dealing with this item, the legal apologist might ask, "If the Gospel accounts of an empty tomb are valid but Jesus was not resurrected, what then happened to His body?"[187] Despite extensive archaeological research and the (possible) identification of the tomb in which the dead Jesus was laid, no remains have ever been discovered. Granted, the resurrection is an "astonishing" event; but, following Greenleaf, this does not preclude its factuality, given that the evidence that the Gospels provide, that is, initial skepticism followed by firsthand visual, aural, and tactile experiences is otherwise "plain and simple" in nature.[188]

Relevance of the Evidence

The last component of the apologetic case concerns the meaning (or "relevance") of the evidence presented. As brought forth above, legal apologists maintain that the resurrection was a literal event that proves the divinity of Jesus on the basis of what He said about Himself, what Jewish prophetic literature said about a prospective Messiah, and the physical circumstances of His entombment.[189] Each of these pieces of evidence, but especially Jesus' own understanding of who He was, supports the assertion that, if it is deemed to be of sufficient weight, the direct and circumstantial evidence leads to the conclusion that Jesus was (and is) the Son of God.

The Criteria for a Verdict

At this juncture in a typical case, the role of the legal apologist in the resurrection case is essentially concluded, and it is up to the hypothetical judge or the jury to render a verdict. As in all legal cases, the judge or jury can rule only that the resurrection of Jesus probably did or did not occur.[190] "When it comes to history, we can only speak of probability,"[191] and in this instance, there is no available physical evidence (genetic material, for example) capable of yielding an absolutely certain conclusion. But the key question for legal apologists is the amount of proof required to reach a judgment.[192] In Anglo-American jurisprudence, the standard of proof in criminal actions is the establishment of a hypothesis "beyond a reasonable doubt," while in civil cases, the standard is the substantially lower "preponderance of the evidence." Recalling Sherlock's *Trial*, the apologete plainly adopted a favorable situation, framing it as a criminal proceeding in which the prosecution had the burden of proving that the witnesses to the resurrection had committed "perjury." The term *apology* implies that the case to be made is, in fact, a defense; so that the burden of proof rests upon skeptics in arguing that the resurrection did not transpire. Montgomery has never specified the amount of proof needed to yield a verdict in the case for (or against) the resurrection. For his part, Clifford is ambiguous. In his thesis on Montgomery's legal apologetic, Clifford first asserted that the civil test, a preponderance of the evidence, is the "more appropriate legal analogy."[193] But he later backed away from the implicit suggestion that a verdict can be reached on the basis of a preponderance (dominance) of the evidence. After concluding the research for his study, he confided,

> The implication that the listener or reader was in the position of a judge or jury to consider

a verdict was too much to claim. This is certainly so for the technical apologetic. It is understandable why the paradigm has functioned this way as traditionally apologetics has sought to lead the listener or reader to a response. However . . . listeners or readers are not in the position of a judge or jury to consider their verdict.[194]

The present writer is sympathetic to Clifford's misgivings. Still, unless the reader is able to come to some judgment, the legal apologies would seem to be academic exercises. It is doubtful that any reader of a legal apologetic for the resurrection enters the "courtroom" without a preformed disposition toward the factuality of a risen Christ. And no matter how open-minded the fact finder may be, he or she cannot be entirely free of bias. In the final analysis, the legal apologetic is capable of influencing both believers and nonbelievers alike, and it is up to them, not the apologist, to determine whether they are capable of rendering the equivalent of a verdict.

7

The Legal Apologetic's Classification Status and Distinctive Features

Approaches, styles, or schools of Christian apologetics have been classified in manifold ways. There is no scholarly consensus concerning the dimensions that should be used to structure a comprehensive classification of high descriptive and explanatory power.[195]

Benjamin Warfield: Five Classes of Apologetics

Writing at the turn of the twentieth century, Benjamin Warfield divided apologetics into five classes: (1) philosophical approaches aimed at the establishment of God's existence; (2) psychological approaches resting on the contention that knowledge of God's existence is innate; (3) approaches that argue for the ontological status of supernatural or divine occurrences; (4) historical apologetics or "Christian evidences"; and, (5) bibliological apologetics that defend the trustworthiness of the Christian Scriptures.[196] Applying Warfield's schema to legal apologetics, we discover that it spans the fourth and fifth categories, taking into account both "Christian evidences" and testimony appearing in the New Testament.

Bernard Ramm: Families of Apologetic Approaches

A more recent and widely cited classification of Christian apologetics was devised by Bernard Ramm as a means of organizing his 1961 text *Varieties of Christian Apologetics*.[197] While Warfield's model hinged upon differences in the functions to which apologetics are put, Ramm's alternative construct distinguished three "families of apologetics" on the basis of their implicit presumptions about the relationship between faith and reason. In the first of these categories, Ramm placed apologetics that stress the uniqueness of the Christian experience. These approaches have little use for natural theology or Christian evidences and take the experience of faith to be its own proof. Ramm cited Pascal and Kierkegaard as members of this group. In Ramm's schema, a second family of apologetics is comprised of systems that stress natural theology as the point at which apologetics should start. Under this heading, Ramm placed both Aquinas and Butler. The third and final class in Ramm's model is composed of approaches that stress revelation as the foundation upon which apologetics must be built, and here he takes Augustine as his prime example. Plainly, Ramm's approach has little utility for classifying legal apologetics, for while this "school" relies upon Christian evidences such as those advocated by Butler, it has only the most remote connection to Aquinas.

John Frame: Epistemological Approaches

The presuppositional apologist John Frame offered an alternative to Ramm in his 1982 essay "Epistemological Approaches to Evangelical Apologetics."[198] Frame first distinguished among "rationalist," "empirical" and "subjectivist" perspectives. He described himself and his fellow presuppositional apologete Gordon Clark as "rationalists," pointed to John Warwick Montgomery as an exemplary "empiricist," and initially argued that there are no subjectivists within the field of evangelical apologetics because they accept an antithesis between true and false religious doctrine. Frame proceeded to relabel the rationalist perspective as "normative," the empirical perspective as "situational," and the subjectivist view as "existential." As Frame's characterization of these approaches as "perspectives" implies, all three of these apologetic stances are valid and useful. He elaborated on this assertion in the context of an ongoing conflict between adherents of the "normative," or presuppositional, perspective and advocates of "situational," or evidentialist, viewpoint.

> In the current debate over apologetics, we must recognize the claim of the presuppositionalists that knowledge is impossible without law and that the ultimate law is the Scripture. We must also grant the claim of the evidentialists that the truth is found through the publicly observable events of nature and history. And we must grant the point made by many that no one will think rightly unless he is psychologically qualified to do so (there is much to be said here about the noetic effects of sin and the illumination of the Holy Spirit). Any of these approaches may be prominent in any particular apologetic encounter; but none will be successful unless the other approaches are also present implicitly.[199]

Frame's moderate contention that the efficacy of the three perspectives is contingent upon the specifics of the "apologetic encounter" at hand was welcome because of the animosity that had arisen between presuppositionalists and evidentialists, represented respectively by Cornelius Van Til and John Warwick Montgomery. When compared to Warfield's apologetic function and Ramm's faith-reason classifications, Frame's "perspectives" has substantially greater relevance for the classification of legal apologetics, which is clearly evidential. But gauging the distance between presuppositionalism, on the one hand and evidentialism on the other, discussion is required. Although there appear to be meaningful differences between normative and situational apologists, there are some signs that the gap between the two positions has narrowed of late and may not have been as large as it has been characterized in the past.

8

The Central Divide in
Contemporary Apologetics

W hether it serves as the central cut in the
articulation of a comprehensive classifica-
tory construct or not, the current apologetic literature recognizes the division between evidential and
presuppositional approaches, and there is a corresponding tendency to use this contradistinction as a
means of constructing or clarifying respective defini-
tions of the two "camps." In his preface to a collection of essays on evidential apologetics at large,
Montgomery emphasized the prospective value of
an evidential methodology for the evangelization of
"reasonable" secularists.

> The essence of this method is never to be
> satisfied with the mere assertion of Christian
> truth (since anyone can make claims), or with
> the critical destruction of a non-Christian

viewpoint (since the fallaciousness of another world-view never establishes the truth of your own), but rather to show the secularist that Christianity alone can offer adequate factual, evidential support for its beliefs.[200]

According to its leading practitioner, then, evidentialist apologists are united by their use of an empirical method of inquiry. They do not seek to prove the existence of God through any means save that of inferences from specific factual evidence.[201] Nor is it necessary to convince the members of the apologist's audience that Christianity is superior to other theistic faiths; that claim is also demonstrable on a factual basis since no other religion was founded by a person of God.[202]

Cornelius Van Til: Presuppositionalism

Derived from a Calvinist theology, the "Westminster school" of apologetics headed by Cornelius Van Til denies both the need for and the ultimate value of evidentialism. In his 1955 text *The Defense of the Faith*, Van Til observed, "The Reformed apologist will frankly admit that his own methodology presupposes the truth of Christian theism."[203] In apologetic situations the presuppositionalist faces "non-Christians" who harbor an entirely different set of premises, a framework or worldview, one that cannot be overturned by discourse without the intervention of the Holy Spirit. "The issue between believers and non-believers in

Christian theism cannot be settled by a direct appeal to 'facts' or 'laws' whose nature and significance is already agreed upon by both parties to the debate," Van Til declared. He then added that "the question is rather as to what the final reference-point is required to make facts 'and' laws 'intelligible."[204] The final reference point, as Van Til saw it, is belief in God, and, even more pointedly, the Christian Triune God. As Cowan would later note, presuppositionalists like Van Til, Gordon Clark, and John Frame have argued transcendentally that "all meaning and thought—indeed every fact—logically presupposes the God of Scripture."[205] While Van Til tends to define presuppositionalism against evidentialism, he also rejected the "classic" approach to proving God's existence, notably through recourse to Aquinas's "Five Ways." He asserted, "The traditional method of apologetics was devised by Roman Catholic theologians and fits their theology."[206] As Van Til's critics have pointed out, the presuppositional argument that he has advocated seems to be a circular construct: the credibility of Christianity's claims, including the resurrection, rests upon the premise that the Scriptures are true. For his part, Van Til acknowledged that presuppositionalist apologetics has little affirmative utility. Instead, its chief function lies in undercutting the "non-Christians'" errant assumptions about the world, or, rather, clearing the noetic barriers grounded in man's sinful nature. According to Van Til, "The natural man . . . knows that he is the creature of God . . . But he suppresses his knowledge of himself as he truly is. He is the man with the iron mask. The true method of apologetics must seek to tear off that iron mask."[207] In the end, the apologist cannot "convert" the non-Christian, but he can pave the way for his acknowledgment of sin, its distortionary influence on his understanding of the world, and, hence, for the reception of God's grace.

John W. Montgomery: Evidentialism

From Montgomery's standpoint, the presuppositonalists have failed to assume the apologetic mission set forth in 1 Peter. In *Faith Founded on Fact*, Montgomery averred that the Westminster school's "flight from 'verification' . . . is a retreat from the apologetic task laid upon all Christians by the apostolic witness itself."[208] Ironically, Montgomery observed at that time, their rejection of a fact-based apologetic created an odd commonality between the presuppositionalists and liberal theologians. More recently, Montgomery has pointed out that the presuppositional apologetic does have a function to perform but that its role is only negative and clarifying. He explained that the Westminster school's apologetics are "negative, in that the contradictions, ill-logic, and shortcomings of non-Christian systems are exposed . . . and clarifying to fully describe the Gospel so that the unbeliever will not reject it through ignorance and misunderstanding."[209] At a later point in time, Montgomery recognized that Van Til had effectively critiqued the central figure of liberal theology, Karl Barth. Discussion of the "evidential-presuppositional" divide resumes in this chapter following an analysis of Steven Cowan's taxonomy of current apologetic methods.

Cowan's Classifications

One of the most recent efforts to organize apologetics into distinct, if not mutually exclusive, categories was undertaken by Steven Cowan. Cowan solicited various essays from practitioners of what he identified as five apologetic "methodologies." In addition to evidentialism and presuppositionalism, Cowan's collection of five explanatory essays encompassed "classic," "cumulative case," and "Reformed epistemology" approaches.[210] Cowan's volume also includes responses to each of these approaches from adherents of alternative methodologies. While his categorical distinctions are based upon variations in methodology, Cowan recognized that groups of scholars have formed around each of them. Thus, for example, Cowan identified Montgomery as a leading proponent of an evidentialist school, and he called upon one of Montgomery's colleagues, Gary Habermas, to present its position. He identified Van Til and Gordon Clark as the salient presuppositionalists, and the task of putting forth its methodological features was completed by John Frame.

While Aquinas's "Five Ways" have fallen from favor, the "classic" or "two-step" apologetic method remains in currency. In his contribution to Cowan's exchange-of-views collection, William Lane Craig explained:

The methodology of classical apologetics was first to present its argument for theism, which aimed to show that God's existence is at least more probable than not, and then to present Christian evidences, probabilistically construed, for God's revelation in Christ. This is the method that I have adopted in my own work. By means of the *kalam* cosmological argument, I have endeavored to show that a Personal Creator of the universe exists. By means of the historical evidence for the resurrection of Jesus, I have tried to show that God revealed himself in Christ.[211]

The Classical Approach

As Cowan commented, in the "classic" apologetic format, not only is the argument twofold, but the order of the presentation also is essential to its integrity.[212] The classical apology first brings the reader/listener to the certain conviction that God exists and then moves to a fact-based argument that Jesus was God's one and only Son.

According to Clifford, while he is clearly an exemplary evidentialist, John Warwick Montgomery occasionally has employed variants of two of Aquinas's proofs, the contingency argument that God is the sole noncontingent being and the argument from intelligent design.[213] Still, Montgomery's core legal apologetic has no room for and no need of the first step in the classic format. The classical proof of God's existence merely yields a philosophical proof that there is a generic god that is hardly distinguishable from the first cause divinity of eighteenth-century Deism.[214] Most importantly, as with all evidential formats, the third component of the legal approach (see chapter 3) proves the divinity of Jesus, the credibility of His message, and, of necessity, the existence of His Father in heaven.[215] From the standpoint of a legal apologetic, the classic approach is at best awkward and potentially misleading.

The Cumulative Case Approach

In Cowan's characterization the "cumulative case" method is "not in any strict sense a formal argument like a proof or any argument from probability."[216] As one of its salient practitioners has put it, the cumulative case method does "not conform to the ordinary pattern of inductive or deductive reasoning."[217] Representing this "school" within Cowan's collection, Paul Feinberg stated that the cumulative case approach does not yield even a probable proof and is, instead, "more like the brief that a lawyer brings, or an explanation that an historian proposes, or an interpretation in literature."[218] In contrast to both the classic and the evidential approaches (including the legal apologetic), the cumulative case does not unfold according to a necessary or even a prototypical sequence of presentation. It assesses the truth of Christianity as a whole, according to a series of tests. Feinberg enumerated seven measures of a religious belief system's validity: (1) consistency (absence of inherent contradictions); (2) correspondence or empirical fit ("with reality"); (3) comprehensive-ness (in explaining good and evil, human nature, and so on); (4) simplicity; (5) livability; (6) fruit-fulness (practical consequences); and (7) conserva-tion (meaning that "when we find some anomaly to our theory, we first choose solutions that require the least radical revision of our view of the world").[219] Although the cumulative case method uses Christian evidences, factuality is but one of several measures through which it attempts to support the argument that the Christian belief system is "true."

The Evidential Approach

There is an evident affinity between Feinberg's cumulative case model and evidential apologetics. Indeed, commenting upon Feinberg's presentation of it, Habermas stated that it "could be considered a sub-species in the camp of evidentialist methodology."[220] In complementary manner, Feinberg allowed that "the cumulative case approach that I have advocated could be seen as an extension or modification of what is called the evidentialist approach."[221] Even more specific to this book's interest, the cumulative case method has been consistently analogized to a legal brief.[222] In his analysis of Montgomery's legal apolo-getic, Clifford wrote that "in laws, it is not necessary for each item of fact to stand on its own as proof of the issue. It is said to be enough if each item of evidence shows the fact in issue is more probable. In a cumulative case therefore each item creates a cord that is one strand of a rope."[223]

Cumulative Case and Legal Apologetics

Despite the points of correspondence, there are substantial differences between cumulative case and legal apologetics. As Feinberg observed, the cumulative case apologists argue that "Christian theism is the best explanation for *all* available evidence *taken together.*"[224] By contrast, the legal apologetic insists that each piece of evidence can be weighed according to a set of specific tests to yield a cumulative weight. Feinberg's method suggests that some of the considerations taken into account may not contribute to the likelihood that the case at hand is valid. Most importantly, the cumulative case approach is exceedingly broad in its scope: it argues that Christianity as a whole is credible. The legal apologetic, by contrast, states that because the resurrection is factually true, Christian belief as a whole is necessarily valid. Unlike the cumulative case, then, in the legal apologetic, the resurrection effectively stands on its own.

Reformed Epistemology and Presuppositionalism

As to the fifth of the views covered by Cowan, the "Reformed epistemology," it is close to the presuppositionalist stance. According to Kelly James Clark, his school takes issue with evidential apologetics. "We are told that if a belief is unsupported by evidence of some kind, it would be irrational to believe it. Reformed epistemology challenges this 'evidentialist' epistemological assumption. Those who advocate this view hold that it is perfectly reasonable for a person to believe many things without evidence."[225] The difference between this stance and that of Van Til, (Gordon) Clark, and Frame is difficult to discern. We can reasonably surmise, however, that the gap between this emerging "school" and legal apologetics is roughly equivalent to the evidentialist-presuppositionalist divide.

A Reassessment of the Central Divide

For more than two decades some scholars have argued that the gap between the presuppositional and evidential apologetic frameworks is not as great as it has been characterized as being.[226] Thus, in his 1984 presentation of a "balanced" approach to apologetics, Ronald Mayers declared, "The debate between evidentialists and presuppositionalists over self-interpreting facts or God-interpreted facts is artificial, since both sides accept and believe that this is a God-created world with a God-sanctioned history."[227] More recently, in a conclusion on the "five-views" exchanges that he moderated, Cowan observed that there is "a growing consensus that the various apologetic methods are not as polarized as they once seemed . . . apologetic methodologists of various schools have been willing to concede views that they once would have opposed."[228] In light of this growing consensus, we may readily inquire if this "convergence" represents an actual shift or merely a rhetorical reconciliation.

Returning to Van Til's position in the mid-1950s, evidential apologists might be taken aback by some of the statements he made at that time. For instance, Van Til stated, "I see induction and analytical reasoning as part of one process of interpretation. I would therefore engage in historical apologetics."[229] Moreover, Van Til even recognized that *"for argument's sake,"* a Christian apologist can adopt a "non-believer's" worldview, including agnostic secular empiricism.[230] Nevertheless, he steadfastly dismissed probability as an inherent feature of historical/evidential apologetics, declaring that "a really fruitful historical apologetic argues that every fact *is* and *must* be such as proves the truth of the Christian theistic position."[231] Van Til did not deign to explain how a historical apologetic could demonstrate the certainty of conclusions drawn from inductive inferences. Considering this, the gap between evidentialism (and the legal apologetic) and presuppositionalism was insurmountable.

In 1994, Frame put forth a much more flexible version of presuppositional apologetics. In this work, Frame initially identified himself as an adherent of "that special kind of Reformed apologetics developed by Cornelius Van Til."[232] But he then proceeded to critique Van Til's work on two counts: (1) his lack of specific arguments and (2) his assertions concerning absolute certainty in the truth of Christian belief.[233] Moving even farther away from Van Til's stance, Frame put forth a brief sketch of an evidential/legal apologetic, writing,

> It is quite legitimate, as we shall see, to argue on the basis of evidence, such as the testimony of the five hundred witnesses to

the Resurrection (1 Cor. 15:6). Eyewitness accounts may be used argumentatively as follows: If Jesus' post-Resurrection appearances are well attested, then the Resurrection is a fact. His post-Resurrection appearances are well attested; therefore, the Resurrection is fact.[234]

He then raised his reservations about this form of argument, contending that this "proof" would still not satisfy a radical or extreme empiricist like Hume, given Hume's categorical rejection of "miracles" as a violation of the natural order.[235] Frame's stance here appears to be transitional. On the one hand, he pulls away from the absolute certainty criteria of Van Til, while on the other, he seems to accept Hume's premise that "miracles" such as the resurrection cannot be well attested.

Responding to Frame's exposition of presuppositionalism in Cowan's collection, Habermas duly noted that Frame is much more open to the acceptance of "hard facts" than Van Til[236] and that the presuppositional "school" to which Frame belongs had moved increasingly closer to evidentialism.[237] Habermas proceeded to suggest that Frame's approach "is better considered a theological outlook on apologetics rather than a distinct apologetic approach."[238] But even in Frame's version, presuppositionalism's concerns about the degree of probability and the quantum of proof required to convince a strict empiricist of the factuality of the resurrection blocks any further movement toward convergence with evidential methods.

In the end, the "great divide" has narrowed, but an evidential apologetic remains distinct from even a revised presuppositional apologetic.

What we may conclude, then, is that evidentialism is a distinct apologetic school in itself; it differs substantially from all other methods of apologetics in circulation. The question then becomes: Does the legal apologetic vary enough from other types of evidential apologetic to be considered a school in its own right?

A Comparison of Historical and Legal Apologetics

In terms of their shared empirical orientation, their common use of Christian evidences, and their historical evolution, there is a strong connection between historical and legal apologetics.[239] Nevertheless, these branches of evidential apologetics do display some significant differences in terms of both the type of evidence that they take into account and the criteria they use to assess its relevance and to reach a judgment. This becomes very apparent when we turn to some representative historical apologetics for the resurrection.

Peter Kreeft and Ronald Tacelli: Historical Data

In their *Handbook of Christian Apologetics*, Peter Kreeft and Ronald Tacelli put forth a "standard" historical apologetic that can be taken as representative of this "school."[240] They first asserted that "Christ's resurrection can be proved with at least as much certainty as any universally believed and well-documented event in ancient history."[241] Although the standard of proof differs from the "reasonable doubt" and/or "preponderance of the evidence" criteria implicit in legal apologetics, this is a comparatively minor disparity, especially given that even among self-identified legal apologists there is no perfect agreement about what quantum of proof is required to render a verdict. But Kreeft and Tacelli then asserted that the thesis that the resurrection occurred does *not* demand the reader's supposition that miracles are possible or even that the Gospel accounts meet any test of admissibility. Instead, they maintained, "We need presuppose only two things, both of which are hard data, empirical data, which no one denies: the existence of the New Testament texts as we have them, and the existence (but not) necessarily the truth of the Christian religion as we find it today."[242] The core of their argument is that Christians continue to celebrate Easter (and Sundays) in commemoration of an extraordinary event that happened two millennia ago and that this celebration is grounded in the belief that Jesus was resurrected.[243] This position is radically different from that of legal apologetics. In this version of historical apologetics, the authenticity of New Testament documents need not be determined, the argument demands no direct eyewitness testimony, and the argument requires no affirmative proof of the empty tomb.

Having established the parameters of their argument, Kreeft and Tacelli enumerated five possible explanations of why Christians currently celebrate

Easter and asked: "Which theory about what really happened in Jerusalem that first Easter Sunday can account for the data?" The first of these theories posits that the resurrection actually happened. The remaining four hypotheses were drawn by the apologetes from skeptical interpretations of Easter's origins: (2) that the apostles were deceived by a hallucination; (3) that the apostles/Gospel writers created a myth that they did not intend to be taken literally; (4) that they created a fictitious story that they meant to foist on the world as an actual occurrence; and, (5) that Jesus did not die on the cross but merely swooned.[244] Kreeft and Tacelli then proceeded to refute each of these four alternative interpretations, and on this basis they concluded that the only remaining thesis must be true in the same sense that other "well-documented events in ancient history" are accepted as true.[245]

Gary Habermas: Minimal Historical Facts

Writing a few years earlier, Gary Habermas first listed a set of universally accepted data about the resurrection in his "minimal-facts" historical apologetic. Rather than the continuance of an Easter tradition in the present, Habermas stated, "The pivotal fact from our list, recognized as historical by virtually all scholars, is the original experiences of the disciples. It is almost always admitted that the disciples had real experiences and that 'something happened.'"[246] Like Kreeft and Tacelli, in this exercise Habermas declared that in contrast to evangelical apologists who attempt to establish the general trustworthiness of the Bible, his "minimal-facts" procedure "does not even require that Scripture have the quality of general trustworthiness."[247] All that is needed to demonstrate the likely factual reality of the resurrection, Habermas claimed, is to refute alternative explanations of why the disciples reacted to the Easter event as they did. "Since this data can be established by critical procedures which utilize the minimal amount of knowable historical facts," Habermas reasoned, "contemporary scholars should not reject such evidence by referring to 'discrepancies' in the NT texts or to its general 'unreliability.'"[248] Here, too, the admissibility of Scripture is not an issue, and there is no effort to establish the credibility of the resurrection accounts given by eyewitnesses other than that their subsequent actions are consistent with having beheld the risen Christ.

In his submission to Cowan's volume, Habermas put forth a somewhat different argument for the factuality of the resurrection.[249] He allowed that perfectly certain conclusions cannot be reached through inferences derived from empirical evidence,[250] yet "it is still possible to reach sturdy conclusions within the canons of historical research."[251] In this essay, Habermas started with Jesus' teachings about Himself. Both Scripture and non-Christian evidence (Josephus) indicate that Jesus taught that He was the Son of God, and His actions (as recorded within the New Testament and implied in non-Christian source material) attest to Jesus' belief in His own deity. Habermas then moved to the issue of whether Jesus actually died, arguing that this is highly probable given the "efficiency" of Roman execution methods (including the spear to ensure death), and from there to the issue of whether He appeared to His followers. He then replicated Kreeft and Tacelli's mode of disproving all naturalistic explanations for the resurrection appearances.[252] Here again, the historical apologete has deliberately sidestepped the objections of modern source critics, contending that his minimal-facts approach "cannot be rejected by someone who does not believe that the New Testament is not a good source."[253] As the final element in his argument, Habermas briefly addressed Cavin's "eternal-revivification" objection, asserting, "It is reasonable to conclude, in light of Jesus' unique claims about himself and the historical likelihood of the resurrection, that he was in the best position to interpret the meaning of this event."[254]

In their recently published *The Case for the Resurrection of Jesus*, Habermas and Michael Licona presented a hybrid of historical and legal apologetics. They cited five principles common to the assessment of historical claims: (1) multiple, independent sources support historical claims; (2) attestation by an enemy supports historical claims; (3) embarrassing admissions support historical claims; (4) eyewitness testimony supports historical claims, and (5) early testimony supports historical claims.[255] Here the apologetes moved away from a "minimal-facts" argument by taking into account eyewitness testimony requiring the assessment of individual and aggregated witnesses' credibility and by including "early testimony" (thereby necessitating the reliability of New Testament documents, the authenticity of their authorship, and the sufficiency of their transmission through a chain of custody). The standard of proof that Habermas and Licona imposed on their argument is somewhat less robust than even the "preponderance-of-evidence" criterion used in civil lawsuits, but there is a broad equivalence. The authors contend that "a position is demonstrated, when the reasons for accepting it 'significantly' outweigh the reasons for not accepting it."[256]

Summary

While the arguments advanced by historical apologists for the resurrection vary among each other, there are meaningful contrasts that can be drawn between their methods in general and those used in explicitly legal apologetics. First, there is much less reliance upon direct, eyewitness accounts of the encounters with the postresurrection Jesus. Historical apologetes tend to draw inferences from the subsequent behavior of Jesus' disciples and from the continuation of the Easter tradition, while they avoid assessment of witness credibility beyond what their subsequent actions imply.[257] Hence, there is no need to apply Greenleaf's "fivefold" test of witness credibility. In complementary manner, the role of circumstantial evidence is much more important in the historical approach than it is in the legal apologetic. Second, while the legal apologist confronts the objections of source critics in arguing for the admissibility of New

Testament documents, apologetes of the historical school tend to circumvent this task. Third, historical approaches tend to use a process of elimination; they establish alternative explanations of the Easter event and its effects, disprove each of them, and arrive at an actual resurrection as the only remaining (or "best") result. Legal apologetics is oriented toward an affirmative defense. Although alternative theories of the evidence are rebutted by legal apologists, the structure of their arguments is directed towards "proving" the (probable) case for the resurrection rather than debunking naturalistic interpretations of inferences drawn from circumstantial data. Lastly, presuming that a legal apologist specifies the quantum of proof required to yield a verdict, the criteria that must be satisfied to reach a judgment is more specific and slightly more demanding than that which historical apologists impose upon themselves.

From all this, we can conclude that a prototypical legal apologetic for the resurrection is, in fact, significantly different from a set of representative historical apologetics for the resurrection. In relation to this study's primary objective, the present writer would now contend that legal apologetics does constitute a distinct school within Christian apologetics.

The final point of inquiry concerns the current efficacy of the legal apologetic. The concluding chapter will focus on the mission of Christian apologetics in light of the challenges that presently confront the faith and its claims about the resurrection.

9

The Relevance and Effectiveness of Legal Apologetics

The Relevance of Legal Apologetics

Christian apologetics performs multiple functions. Its core mission includes defending the trustworthiness of Scripture from explicit assaults mounted by "non-Christians," highlighting the continuing value of the Christian message within a given intellectual/cultural environment, clarifying orthodox beliefs against heretical interpretations, facilitating evangelism, and bolstering the faith of believers. As was brought forth earlier, the historical trajectory of Christian apologetics exhibits powerful and consistent correlations between the level of apologetic activity and apologetic innovation, on the one hand, and the appearance of external challenges, such as Neoplatonism, Islamic Aristotlianism, Deism, and modern source criticism, on the other. While the Gospel message is eternal, apologetics has necessarily adapted to specific historical conditions that exert a strong influence upon the relative usefulness of any given approach.

Since the Enlightenment, Protestant apologists have routinely issued calls for a revitalization of apologetic activity, and the first decade of the twenty-first century is no exception. Thus, for example, John Warwick Montgomery has recently declared that while apologetics is "not a universally valued task," there is a "crying need for a dynamic use of a viable apologetic."[258] Understandably, in Montgomery's estimation, evidential apologetics is capable of responding to that need and the legal apologetic school with which he is associated offers a superior means of addressing the challenges and opportunities at hand. In this context, we recall Dulles's observation that in the modern era, "apologetics came to recognize that every Christian harbors within himself a secret infidel."[259] In the present writer's estimation, while apologetics retains a number of purposes, its most pressing function lies in counteracting the influence of liberal theology, existentialism, secularism, cultural relativism, and postmodernism on self-identified Christian believers. In fact, these influences are so pervasive that the "typical" believer may not even be aware that he or she is susceptible to their effects.

There is variation among apologetic schools concerning the role that apologetics can and should play. Once again, the sharpest division on this count is between presuppositionalists and evidentialists. From Van Til's viewpoint, attempting to reason with nonbelievers is ultimately futile. "The unqualified acceptance of the authority of Christ speaking in Scripture," Van Til wrote, "so far from excluding the possibility of fruitful discussion with unbelievers, is rather the only possible foundation for it."[260] The practical problem, of course, is that the "man in the iron mask" may not realize that he is so encumbered. He is not likely to appreciate efforts by apologists to lift the veil. And he is, therefore, powerfully predisposed against considering any argument that embodies the premise that he is not only wrong about religion (and, in fact, the nature of all reality) but that these errors also stem from sin. Although more enlightened presuppositionalists—Frame for example—have modified claims to absolute certainty, contemporary adherents of this approach still hold that the primary aim of apologetics is to free "nonbelievers" from the shackles of sinful cognitions.[261]

This position stands in sharp relief with evidential/legal apologetics.[262] No preliminary hearings are required before the evidential/legal apologist puts forth his or her case. Legal apologetics is affirmatively oriented. While it must respond to alternative theories about the faith and its central event in the resurrection, legal apologetics aims at the constructive goal of showing that the New Testament's accounts of the first Easter and its immediate aftermath are (in all probability) factually true.[263]

Current Challenges

While the issuance of a specific attack on Christian beliefs (Celsus's *True Doctrine,* for example) has served as catalyst to apologetic activity, the underlying challenges that apologists have confronted have been broad and persistent. In 1967, Clark Pinnock noted that the credibility of orthodox Christianity was still being challenged by the existential philosophy traceable to the early nineteenth century by a theological liberalism that had been active for the better part of a century, as well as by scriptural criticism /quest for the historical Jesus with roots that extend back to the Enlightenment.[264] As Pinnock saw it, the subjectivism of Kierkegaard's existential Christianity had been extended through Barth and Bultmann to become an embedded feature of liberal theology.[265] Rather than repudiating religious irrationalism and its assertion that Christianity can be understood as a purely subjective phenomenon leaving each believer "free" to pursue his or her ideas about Christianity independent of the Gospels was ensconced within modern theology. The factuality of Christianity was not merely denied; it was deemed irrelevant.[266] All of this occurred during a historical era in which secularism gained regency "with the result that what is 'real' is the profane, a contingent world without purpose, and a smothering relativity."[267] This was not a straightforward attack on the core beliefs of Christianity. As Pinnock observed, although the bulk of the American populace still reported a belief in some kind of God and even admired Jesus as a moral teacher, surveys had consistently indicated that "people clearly believe in the *practical* irrelevance of the gospel."[268]

Pinnock was by no means the only Christian apologist to see the pervasive nature of this threat and its diffusion within Christian thought. In his 1970 treatise, *The Suicide of Christian Theology*, Montgomery argued that in its effort to "make peace with the relativism of the contemporary mind," many Christian leaders had embraced an amorphous ecumenicalism from which the consideration of Scripture was almost entirely absent.[269] Montgomery vigorously expounded on this point, writing, "Contemporary theologians have destroyed themselves by their unnecessary and unwarranted destruction of biblical revelation on which all sound theology is based. The only hope for a resurrected theology lies in a recovery of confidence in the historical Christ and in the Scriptures He stamped with approval as God's Word."[270] Ironically, even as liberal theology underwent fusion with relativism, the environment in which Christianity operates became increasingly diverse. In *Faith Founded on Fact*, Montgomery commented upon the implications of a pluralistic society for the fulfillment of the Greater Commandment.

> The twentieth-century world, growing steadily smaller as the communication revolution continues, displays a religious pluralism experientially unknown to our grandfathers and remarkably similar to the heterogeneous religious situation in the Roman Empire during

the first century. Sects and cults proliferate; philosophies of life, explicit and implicit, vie for our attention; and older, previously dormant religions, such as Buddhism and Islam, are engaged in vigorous proselytising. All about us ultimate concerns spring up, each claiming to be more ultimate, more worthy of our total commitment, than the other. In the university world the pluralistic cacophony is louder than perhaps anywhere else: materialism, idealism, pragmatism, communism, hedonism, mysticism, existentialism, and a hundred other options present themselves to the college student in classrooms, bull-sessions, student organizations, political rallies, and social activities.[271]

To be sure, the allied notions that all belief systems are equally valid and that Christianity is especially retrograde in its insistence on the possession of an absolute truth were actively challenged by popular Christian apologists like Josh McDowell. Indeed, there has been a sustained rise in Christian evangelism during the past quarter century. This work continues apace, yet the basic challenges remain in place.

In the preface to a 2006 study guide covering the field, H. Wayne House and Joseph Holden reported that Christian apologetics was currently suffering through difficult times and asserted that dogmatic presuppositionalism had alienated a large segment of the populace from apologetics at large. House and Holden then pointed to the ascendance of "a post-modern or existential mind-set in which truth as an objective reality is really not knowable."[272] In contrast to modern relativism and secularism, this postmodern philosophy in its deconstructionist form does not merely deny the possibility of finding truth; it denies truth altogether. As Feinberg has observed, within the current intellectual climate of Western civilization deconstructionism maintains that there is no truth at all, not simply that the human mind is incapable of grasping the truth.[273] "If any form of post-modernism like deconstructionism is true," Feinberg realized, "then there can be no task for apologetics and discussions about defending the faith are meaningless."[274] At bottom, postmodern deconstructionists are self-contradictory hypocrites; while denying belief in truth and good and evil, they "continue to act in ways that presuppose them in practice."[275] Evidentialists like Habermas[276] and presuppositionalists like Frame[277] are united in their identification of postmodernism as the latest challenge to the faith.

The Effectiveness of Legal Apologetics

In the present writer's estimation, a legal apologetic for the resurrection is especially relevant to the circumstances of the day and is therefore likely to have greater effectiveness than alternative apologetic approaches in addressing them. To begin, the legal apologetic (and, indeed, all evidential apologetics) is uncompromising in its insistence on the full claims of the New Testament. As Teh has put it, "The Christian faith declares that the truth of its absolute claims rest squarely on certain historical facts, always open to investigation."[278] Christianity does not declare that Jesus' followers had some type of paranormal experience on the first Easter; it asserts that they witnessed the risen Christ in the flesh. While the legal apologetic recognizes that the available data enables modern Christians to reach a probable finding of the facticity of the resurrection, it does not argue that the eyewitnesses of the New Testament had a probable experience but instead that they saw, heard, and felt a miraculous event through the same sensory-cognitive apparatus through which human beings experience and interpret mundane events. In courts of law, arguments are presented from facts, and while their validity is questionable, their purported status as facts is not. With virtually no exceptions, judicial decision makers do not have the benefit of observing these facts as they occur; they must rely upon accounts formulated in the past. As Clifford has observed, "Law is a craft that tackles the past."[279] In this regard, both historical and legal apologetics are suited to the mission of defending Christianity in its full claim to actuality.[280]

As noted near the outset of chapter 2, the New Testament writers utilized legal rhetorical forms and presented evidence in a manner that would have been admissible in Jewish, Greek, and Roman courts or forums. Both the Old and the New Testaments are replete with references to the law: the Torah itself was the basic law of Jewish people, and Jesus and His disciples appeared before formal tribunals.[281] Despite the rise of philosophical apologetics among the early church fathers, the exchanges of the first Christian apologetes with "nonbelievers" (committed adversaries and prospective converts alike) relied heavily upon the presentation of evidence to individuals who used the criteria of ancient judicial practice to assess its credibility.[282] Not only does the legal apologetic school have an established tradition, but also it is arguably coextensive with Christianity itself. While apologetics must adapt to changing conditions, this connection to biblical times underscores the durability of legal apologetics.

According to Francis Beckwith, another strength of legal apologetics stems from the law's development of "meticulous legal standards in distinguishing truth from error."[283] As Johnson and others have remarked, "Most modern juridical apologists have operated in common-law based nations."[284] In contrast to the positive legal systems of Western Europe, the rules, tests, and criteria found in common-law societies were not imposed by statute; they came into being through the accumulation of practice and precedent, through experience.[285] To some extent, this is a departure from the pattern through which the standards of modern historical research have evolved, that is, through the adoption of yardsticks from philosophy, physical sciences, and, later, allied social sciences. To this day, while historians embrace a variety of measures for assessing the truth, judicial bodies are obligated to employ unified standards that are universally recognized within the respective national judicial systems. Moreover, as the prominence of the ancient-document and parol-evidence rules in the legal apologetical literature indicates, "a strength of the legal apologetic is the law's familiarity with documents and the criteria developed as to their admissibility, interpretation, and credibility."[286]

Although law is sometimes viewed as a mysterious field, virtually everyone in modern society has at least some familiarity with its basic ground rules. "The appeal of the legal apologetic," Clifford has commented, "is the common usage of the legal paradigm."[287] As Montgomery observed in 1975, "The lawyer endeavors to reduce societal conflicts by arbitrating conflicting truth-claims."[288] Conflicting truth-claims are everywhere. They can be observed in political debates, scientific forums, and playing fields. Such concepts as burden of proof and the superiority of eyewitness testimony to hearsay are virtually universal in Western society. So deeply are legal concepts, procedures, and rules ingrained in modern life that they are difficult to jettison since cohesive alternatives to the law are not available.[289] "Apologetically," Montgomery declared, "the modern man faced with the legally grounded evidence for Christ's claims is in the awkward position of having to go to the Cross or throw away the only accepted method of arbitrating ultimate questions in society."[290] As this observation implies, not only are legal analogies employed across a diverse range of contexts, but the law also is used in decisions that have the gravest importance, in matters of life and death. Christian doctrine maintains that the acceptance of Jesus as God's only Son is essential to the believer's ultimate fate throughout eternity. As a recognized decision-making system, only the law approximates dealing with issues of this weight.

Lastly, when set alongside classical "two-step" apologetics, legal arguments for the factual truth of the resurrection are far more accessible.[291] Modern readers are likely to encounter difficulty in attempting to grasp the apologetic arguments of Augustine, Anselm, and Aquinas.[292] Much the same can be said of presuppositional apologetics. Granted, the core of Van Til's argument—that individuals should believe in the facticity of Scripture because it comes from God—is easy enough to understand. But when the reader looks beneath this normative claim, he or she encounters a bewildering array of theological precepts. At bottom, it is difficult for the common reader to follow the arguments advanced in the presuppositional literature since the justification of their approach involves theological abstractions. By contrast, as Clifford commented in the first chapter of his thesis on Montgomery's legal apologetic, "It is aimed at a popular audience as well as academics and fellow lawyers . . . [And] it is also apparent from Montgomery's writings that whilst he adopts a technical legal apologetic he has the 'lay' reader in mind as his argument is not immersed in deep, unexplained, legal jargon."[293] In the hands of a skilled author, the rationale for and operations of a legal apologetic can be reduced to colloquial terms without great violence to its nuances.

If, as the current writer has argued, the present apologetic situation is characterized less by the need to address targeted critiques and more by the need to counteract the influence of subjectivism, secularism, and pluralism upon the common man, the strengths of the legal apologetic are especially relevant. The legal paradigm acknowledges the limitations of the human mind even as it deals with what are presumed to be concrete facts. It does so without sacrificing the essential tenets of Christianity, notably the factual truth of the risen Christ. In its insistence that a conclusive verdict should be rendered by each believer, it countervails the notion that all belief systems can remain equally valid. At bottom, a legal apologetic is eminently suited to meet the challenges of modern society.

Two Disadvantages of Legal Apologetics

From the present writer's perspective, there are two modest disadvantages involved in relying upon a judicial approach to demonstrating the credibility of Christian belief. First, while lawyers are skilled in formulating clear-cut, logical arguments, they are not above making things unnecessarily complicated and engaging in sophistry. A prime example of this can be discerned in the atheist lawyer Richard Packham's (1998) critique of John Warwick Montgomery's "The Jury Returns."[294] A salient element in Packham's essay was his claim that the New Testament does not satisfy the "ancient-document" rule because the latter requires that such materials be signed by their respective authors.[295] As Pehrson would subsequently argue, this stipulation is not an element of the ancient document rule.[296] Even if it were, the Gospel accounts bear the names of their authors and we have no evidence that attributions of authorship are in any way errant. Other scholars, James Holding, for example, have pointed out the defects in Packham's disingenuous critique of "The Jury Returns."[297] Still, this exchange illustrates that individuals who lay claim to expertise in the law can use legal arguments to undercut apologetic defenses in a manner that defies detection by the average reader.

More significantly, as Frame noted in his response to Habermas's presentation of an evidential apologetic, "The attitude of many people today is that, whatever Habermas and other apologists may say there must be some explanation of the data other than the traditional Christian explanation."[298] Admittedly, there is a level of skepticism that the legal apologetic simply cannot penetrate on its own accord. No argument for the factuality of the resurrection could possibly convince Hume of its status as fact. By the same token, as Feinberg has observed, to the extent that postmodern deconstructionists insist that there is no truth whatsoever, all apologetics are limited in their reach. In such instances, no form of apologetics, including efforts to "lift the mask," are apt to succeed. Yet as it now stands, it is not this nucleus of committed ideologues that represents the audience that apologists must address. It is, instead, that much larger segment of the populace that is subject to their pernicious influence, and it is in working with the unconvinced and the wavering, rather than the defiant, that legal apologetics is bound to show a superior efficacy.

Conclusion

As some apologetic scholars have attested, the evidence for the resurrection of Jesus is "quite good," and when presented through the commonsense procedures developed over centuries of legal practice, it forms the basis for a compelling argument.[299] Legal apologetics is eminently qualified to make that argument. It is a school in its own right with distinctive features that enhance its efficacy. Nearly two decades ago, Gary Habermas enumerated five stances toward the ontological status of the resurrection. As might be expected, Habermas endorsed the evidential view that Jesus' rising from the dead is, in all probability, a hard fact. He then wondered: "Is it simply coincidence that this level of evidence is available for this event?"[300] On one level, an answer to this inquiry cannot be framed. On another level, Jesus Himself said that His impending resurrection would serve as a sign of His divinity and, by extension, the truth of the gospel. Among believers, it is not all that far-fetched to believe that the sheer concentration of information that we possess about the resurrection is a direct result of God's intentions. If the thesis advanced in this work is sound, we can further speculate that renewed interest in a legal apologetic under the conditions of our day is also a reflection of Jesus' ministry and His Father's design.

GLOSSARY OF TERMS

Anthropocentric: regarding the human being as the central fact of the universe or assuming the human to be the final aim and end of the Universe.

Circumstantial Evidence: proof of facts offered as evidence from which other facts are to be inferred.

Epistemology: a branch of philosophy that investigates the origin, nature, methods, and limits of human knowledge.

Enlightenment: a philosophical movement of the 18th century, characterized by belief in the power of human reason and by innovations in political, religious, and educational doctrine.

Evidentialism: an emphasis on evidence from the Scriptures.

Fideist: the presentation of Christianity as *factual*— as supportable or verifiable by the reliance in religious matters upon faith, with consequent rejection of appeals to science or philosophy

Gnostic: a member of certain sects among the early Christians who claimed to have superior knowledge of spiritual matters, and explained the world as created by powers or agencies arising as emanations from the Godhead.

Legal Apologetics: a branch of Christian apologetics that affirms that the available evidence to defend Christianity argues for the veracity of the historical and central claims of Christianity when Western legal standards of weighing evidence are applied.

Metaphysics: the underlying theoretical principles of a subject or field of inquiry.

Minimal Facts Approach: the minimal facts approach is a method of proving the resurrection of Christ using only the minimal amount of historical facts which meet the following criteria: they are well evidenced and nearly every scholar accepts them even those who are skeptical.

Neo-Platonism: is the modern term for a school of religious and mystical philosophy that took shape in the 3rd century AD, founded by Plotinus and based on the teachings of Plato and earlier Platonists.

Noumenal: an object as it is in itself independent of the mind, as opposed to a phenomenon. Also called *thing-in-itself.*

Parol Evidence Rule: The parol evidence rule is a principle that preserves the integrity of written documents or agreements by prohibiting the parties from attempting to alter the meaning of the written document through the use of prior and contemporaneous oral or written declarations that are not referenced in the document.

Phenominal: relating to or being a phenomenon: as known through the senses rather than through thought or intuition. (scientific reason)

Presuppositionalism: may be defined as insistence on an ultimate category of thought or a conceptual framework which one must assume in order to make a sensible interpretation of the facts of Christian beliefs. Otherwise any effort to discuss Christian belief is futile.

Probability: that which is likely to be; and that which is most consonant to reason.

Notes

1. John Warwick Montgomery, *The Law above the Law. Why the Law Needs Biblical Foundations/ How Legal Thought Supports Christian Truth* (Minneapolis: Bethany House, 1975).

2. John Warwick Montgomery, *Human Rights and Human Dignity* (Grand Rapids: Zondervan, 1986); John Warwick Montgomery, "Neglected Apologetic Styles: The Juridical and the Literary," in *Evangelical Apologetics,* ed. Michael Bauman, David Hall, and Robert Newman (Camp Hill, PA: Christian Publications, 1996), 119-33; John Warwick Montgomery, "The Jury Returns: A Juridical Defense of Christianity," in *Christians in the Public Square,* ed. C.E.B. Cranfield, David Kilgour, and John Warwick Montgomery (Edmonton, AB: Canadian Institute for Law, Theology and Public Policy, 1996), 223-50. "The Jury Returns" is reproduced in John Warwick Montgomery, ed., *Evidence for Faith: Deciding the God Question* (Edmonton, AB: Canadian Institute for Law, Theology and Public Policy, 2004), 319-41.

3. Hugo Grotius, *The Truth of the Christian Religion*, trans. John Clarke. (Whitefish, MT: Kessinger Publishing, 2004).

4. Simon Greenleaf, *The Testimony of the Evangelists: The Gospels Examined by the Rules of Evidence* (Grand Rapids: Kregel Classics, 1995).

5. Francis Wharton, "Recent Changes in Jurisprudence and Apologetics," *The Princeton Review*: 2(1), (July-December, 1878), 149.

6. Philip Johnson, "Juridical Apologetics 1600-2000 AD: A Bio-Bibliographical Essay," *Global Journal of Classical Theology*: 3(1) (March, 2002), 1.

7. Ross Clifford, *John Warwick Montgomery's Legal Apologetic: An Apologetic for All Seasons.* (Bonn: Verlag for Kultur und Wissenschaft), 267.

8. Ibid., 11.

9. Henry Hock Guan Teh. "Legal Apologetics: Principles of Legal Evidence as Applied to the Quest for Religious Truth," *Global Journal of Classical Theology*: 5(1) (July, 2005), n.p.

10. Johnson, "Juridical Apologetics," 15.

11. Craig Hazen, "Ever Hearing but Never Understanding: A Response to Mark Hutchins's Critique of John Warwick Montgomery's Historical

Apologetics," *Global Journal of Classical Theology*: *3*(1), March, 2002), 3.

12. John Warwick Montgomery, *History and Christianity: A Vigorous, Convincing Presentation of the Evidence for a Historical Jesus* (Minneapolis: Bethany House, 1964).

13. Hazen, "Ever Hearing," 3.

14. Clifford, *Montgomery's Legal Apologetic,* 12.

15. Ibid., 11

16. Ibid..

17. Johnson, "Juridical Apologetics," 1.

18. Ibid..

19. Ibid., 8.

20. Avery Dulles, *A History of Apologetics* (1971; repr., Eugene, OR: Wipf and Stock, 1999), 133-34,140.

21. Kenneth D. Boa and Robert M, Bowman, *Faith Has Its Reasons: An Integrative Approach to Defending Christianity* (Colorado Springs: NavPress, 2001), 161-69.

22. Johnson, "Juridical Apologetics," 2-3.

23. Clifford, *Montgomery's Legal Apologetic,* 19.

24. William Dyrness, *Christian Apologetics in a World Community.* (Downers Grove, IL: Inter-Varsity Press, 1983), 23.

25. Montgomery, *The Law above the Law,* 84.

26. Johnson, "Juridical Apologetics," 1.

27. Gary R. Habermas, "Greg Bahnsen, John Warwick Montgomery, and Evidential Apologetics," *Global Journal of Classical Theology: 3*(1), (March, 2002).

28, Steven B. Cowan,. Introduction to *Five Views on Apologetics,* ed. Steven B. Cowan. (Grand Rapids: Zondervan, 2000), 7-20.

29. Clifford, *Montgomery's Legal Apologetic,* 25.

30. Dyrness, *Christian Apologetics,* 12.

31. Dulles, *History of Apologetics,* xvii.

32. Ibid., 1.

33. Ibid., 13

34. Benjamin B. Warfield, "Apologetics," http://www/reformed.org/apologetics/index.html.

35. Dulles, *History of Apologetics,* 19.

36. Allison Trites, *The New Testament Concept of Witness* (Cambridge: Cambridge University Press, 1977), 133-35.

37. Clifford, *Montgomery's Legal Apologetic,* 19.

38. Ibid., 229.

39. Dulles, *History of Apologetics,* 12.

40. Dyrness, *Christian Apologetics,* 24.

41. Ibid., 25.

42. Clifford, *Montgomery's Legal Apologetic,* 19.

43. J. Duncan M. Derret, *Law in the New Testament* (London: Durton, Longman, and Todd, 1970), 461-63.

44. Bruce W. Winter, "Official Proceedings and Forensic Speeches in Acts 24-26," in *The Book of Acts in Its Ancient Literary Settings,* ed. Bruce W. Winter and Andrew D. Clarke (Grand Rapids: Eerdmans, 1994), 333-36; Allister E. McGrath, "Apologetics to the Romans," *Bibliotheca Sacra 155* (October-December, 1998), 390-91; Clifton Black, *The Rhetoric of the Gospel: Theological Artistry in the Gospels and Acts* (St. Louis: Chalice, 2001), 115-33.

45. Montgomery, "The Jury Returns," in *Evidence for Faith*, 320.

46. Trites, *New Testament Concept of Witness*, 129.

47. Ibid., 135.

48. Clifford, *Montgomery's Legal Apologetic*, 232.

49. William Lane Craig, *The Historical Argument for the Resurrection of Jesus During the Deist Controversy* (Lewiston: Edwin Mellen, 1985), pp.15-16.

50. Trites, *New Testament Concept of Witness*, 79.

51, Clifford, *Montgomery's Legal Apologetic*, 234.

52. Dulles, *History of Apologetics*, 26.

53. Origen. *Origen Contra Celsum*, trans. Henry Chadwick, 2nd ed. (Cambridge: University Press, 1965).

54. Dulles, *History of Apologetics*, 35.

55. Origen, *Contra Celsum*, 3:33.

56. Tertullian. *Apology*, trans. Emily Joseph Daly (New York: Fathers of the Church Inc., 1950).

57. Dulles, *History of Apologetics*, 42.

58. Tertullian, *Apology,* 36.

59. Dulles, *History of Apologetics,* 45.

60. Ibid.

61. Ibid., 71.

62. Ibid., 62.

63. N. Andrew Hoffecker, "Augustine, Aquinas and the Reformers," in *Building a Christian World View: Volume 1, God, Man and Knowledge*, ed. W. Andrew Hoffecker and Gary Scott Smith (Phillipsburg, NJ: Presbyterian and Reform Publishing, 1986), 238.

64. Ibid.,.239.

65. Dulles, *History of Apologetics,* 62.

66. John Warwick Montgomery. *A History of Apologetics through the Centuries.* Newburgh, IN: Trinity College and Seminary, n.d), 27.

67. Dulles, *History of Apologetics,* 111.

68. Ibid., 80.

69. Dyrness, *Christian Apologetics,* 31.

70. Dulles, *History of Apologetics,* 77.

71. Hoffecker, "Augustine, Aquinas and the Reformers," 235.

72. Ibid., 246.

73. Thomas Aquinas, *Summa contra Gentiles: Book Three: Providence, Part 1*, trans. Vernon J. Bourke (Notre Dame, IN: University of Notre Dame Press, 1975), p.33.

74. Hoffecker, "Augustine, Aquinas and the Reformers," 246ff.

75. Dulles, *History of Apologetics*, 91.

76. Ibid., 113.

77. Dyrness, *Christian Apologetics*, 35.

78. Dulles, *History of Apologetics*, 113.

79. Montgomery, *A History of Apologetics*, p.33.

80. Hoffecker, "Augustine, Aquinas and the Reformers," 25.

81. Clifford, *Montgomery's Legal Apologetic*, 247.

82. John Warwick Montgomery, *Faith Founded on Fact: Essays in Evidential Apologetics* (Newburgh, IN: Trinity College and Seminary, 1978), xii.

83. Johnson, "Juridical Apologetics," 2.

.

84. Clifford, *Montgomery's Legal Apologetic,* 21.

85. Grotius, *Truth of the Christian Religion*, 80.

86. Ibid., 84-85.

87. Dulles, *History of Apologetics,* 134.

88. Montgomery, *A History of Apologetics*, p.34

89. Dulles, *History of Apologetics,* 134.

90. Blaise Pascal, *Pensees.* trans. A.J. Krailsheimer, rev. ed. (London: Penguin Books, 1995), no.309, p.97.

91. Ibid., no.307, p.95.

92. Ibid., no.298, p.94.

93. Dyrness, *Christian Apologetics,* 38.

94. Ibid.

95. Dulles, *History of Apologetics,* 139-40.

96. Craig, *The Historical Argument,* 234-35

97) Montgomery, *A History of Apologetics*, p.35.

98. Hoffecker, "Augustine, Aquinas and the Reformers," 249.

99. Montgomery, *A History of Apologetics,* p.38.

100. Herman S. Reimarus, "Concerning the Intention of Jesus and His Teachings," in *Reimarus Fragments,* ed. Charles H. Talbert; trans. Ralph S. Fraser. (London: SCN, 1971), 176.

101. Clifford, *Montgomery's Legal Apologetic,* 29.

102. Dulles, *History of Apologetics,* 144.

103. Joseph Butler, *The Analogy of Religion Natural and Revealed to the Constitution and Course of Nature* (1736; repr. New York: Ungar, 1961).

104. Dulles, *History of Apologetics,* 140.

105. Butler, *Analogy of Religion,* 3.

106. Ibid., 213.

107. Dyrness, *Christian Apologetics,* 41.

108. Butler, *Analogy of Religion,* 243.

109. Ibid., 244.

110. Montgomery, *A History of Apologetics,* p.37

111. Dulles, *History of Apologetics*, 143.

112. Butler, *Analogy of Religion*, 142.

113. Thomas Sherlock, *The Tryal of the Witnesses of the Resurrection of Jesus* (London: J. Roberts, 1729). This source is reproduced in John Warwick Montgomery, ed., *Jurisprudence: A Book of Readings*. Strasbourg: International Scholarly Publications, 1974), 339-450.

114. Sherlock, *Tryal* (1729), 62.

115. Johnson, "Juridical Apologetics," 3.

116. William Paley, *A View of the Evidences of Christianity* (1794; repr. London: Longmans, 1830), 364.

117. Ibid., 366.

118. Clifford, *Montgomery's Legal Apologetic*, 28.

119. Craig, *The Historical Argument*, 352.

120. Dulles, *History of Apologetics*, 158.

121. Soren Kierkegaard, *Philosophical Fragments*, trans. D.F. Swenson (Princeton: Princeton University Press, 1941); Soren Kierkegaard, *On Authority and Revelation*, trans. Walter Lowrie. (Princeton: Princeton University Press, 1955).

122. Gary Habermas, "Jesus' Resurrection and Contemporary Criticism: An Apologetic." *Criswell Theological Review*: *4*(1) (1989): 165.

123. Dulles, *History of Apologetics,* 165.

124. Kierkegaard, *On Authority*, 59.

125. Clark H. Pinnock, *Set Forth Your Case: An Examination of Christianity's Credentials*. (Chicago: Moody, 1967), 27.

126. David Friedrich Strauss, *Life of Jesus*, trans. George Eliot (London, 1846).

127. Dulles, *History of Apologetics,* 163.

128. Johnson, "Juridical Apologetics," 6.

129. Ibid.

130. Clifford, *Montgomery's Legal Apologetic,* 22.

131. Montgomery, 1975, p.85.

132. Greenleaf, *Testimony of the Evangelists,* 11.

133. Ibid., 12.

134. Ibid., 16.

135. Ibid., 17.

136. Ibid., 28.

137. Ibid., 31.

138. Ibid., 36.

139. Clifford, *Montgomery's Legal Apologetic*, 23.

140. Ibid..

141. Dulles, *History of Apologetics*, 157.

142. Ibid., 185-86.

143. Montgomery, *A History of Apologetics*, p.43.

144. Ibid.

145. Dulles, *History of Apologetics*, 198.

146. Warfield, "Apologetics," n.p.

147. Ibid.

148. Dulles, *History of Apologetics*, 198.

149. Ibid.,.212.

150. Charles R. Morrison, *Proofs of Christ's Resurrection from a Lawyer's Standpoint* (Andover: Warren F. Draper, 1882); Joseph Evans Sagebeer, *The Bible in Court* (Philadelphia: Lippincott, 1900);

Francis J. Lamb, *Miracle and Science: Biblical Miracles Examined by the Methods, Rules, and Tests of the Science of Jurisprudence as Administered Today in Courts of Justice* (Oberlin, OH: Bibliotheca Sacra, 1909); Walter Chandler, *The Trial of Jesus from a Lawyer's Standpoint* (New York: Federal Press, 1925); Stephen Williams, *The Bible in Court or Truth v. Error* (Dearborn, MI, Dearborn Press, 1925); Howard Hyde Russell, *A Lawyer's Examination of the Bible* (Westerville, OH: Bond, 1935); Irwin H. Linton, *A Lawyer Examines the Bible: An Introduction to Christian Evidences,* 5th ed. (Boston: W.A. Wilde, 1943).

151. Willard Sperry, *"Yes, But—." The Bankruptcy of Apologetics* (New York: Harper, 1931).

152. Dulles, *History of Apologetics,* xvii.

153. Karl Barth, *Church Dogmatics*, trans. G.W. Bromley and T.F. Torrance (Edinburgh: T & T Clark, 1956).

154. Habermas, "Jesus' Resurrection," 163.

155. Rudolph Bultmann, *Theology of the New Testament*, trans. K Goebel. (New York: Scribner's, 1951).

156, Rudolph Bultmann, *Kerygma and Myth: A Theological Debate*, trans. R.H. Fuller (London: Austin Farrer, 1953), 207.

157. Ibid.

158. Edward John Carnell I*ntroduction to Christian Apologetics*. (Grand Rapids: Eerdmans, 1948).

159. Montgomery, *A History of Apologetics,* 45.

160. Cornelius Van Til, *The Defense of the Faith* (Phillipsburg, NJ: Presbyterian and Reformed Publishing, 1955).

161. Dulles, *History of Apologetics,* xvii.

162. Paul Althaus. *The So-Called Kerygma and the Historical Jesus*, trans. David Cairns (London: Oliver & Boyd. 1959), 34.

163. Clifford, *Montgomery's Legal Apologetic,* 40.

164. Habermas, "Jesus' Resurrection," 159.

165. Teh, "Legal Apologetics," n.p.

166. Montgomery, *A History of Apologetics,* 18.

167. Gary R. Habermas, "Evidential Apologetics," in *Five Views on Apologetics,* ed. Steven B. Cowan (Grand Rapids: Zondervan, 2000), 92.

168. Robert Gregg Cavin, "Is There Sufficient Historical Evidence to Establish the Resurrection

of Jesus?" *Faith and Philosophy*: *12*(3)(July, 1995): 361.

169. Gerard Chrispin, *The Resurrection: The Unopened Gift* (Epson, Surrey: Day One Publications, 1999), 56.

170. Gary R. Habermas and Michael R. Licona, *The Case for the Resurrection of Jesus* (Grand Rapids: Kregel, 2004), 27.

171. Clifford, *Montgomery's Legal Apologetic*, 255.

172. Montgomery, "The Jury Returns," in *Evidence for Faith*, 334.

173. Ibid., 336.

174. Habermas and Licona, *Case for the Resurrection*, 28.

175. Gary Habermas, "Jesus' Resurrection and Contemporary Criticism: An Apologetic" (Part II), *Criswell Theological Review*: *4*(2) (1990): 383.

176. Montgomery, *The Law above the Law*, 87.

177. Ibid.

178. Ibid., 87-88.

179. Ibid., 88.

180. Ibid., 89.

181. Clifford, *Montgomery's Legal Apologetic,* 110.

182. Greenleaf, *Testimony of the Evangelists,* 31.

183. Montgomery, *Human Rights and Human Dignity,* 131-60; Montgomery, "Neglected Apologetic Styles," 269-82.

184. Clifford, *Montgomery's Legal Apologetic,* 57.

185. Ibid..

186. Montgomery, "The Jury Returns," in *Evidence for Faith,* 323.

187. Clifford, *Montgomery's Legal Apologetic,* 44.

188. Greenleaf, *Testimony of the Evangelists,* 36.

189. Clifford, *Montgomery's Legal Apologetic,* 41.

190. Ibid., 46-47.

191. Habermas and Licona, *Case for the Resurrection,* 31.

192. Clifford, *Montgomery's Legal Apologetic,* 50.

193. Ibid., 51.

194. Ibid., 55.

195. Cky J. Carrigan, "Contemporary Evangelical Approaches to Apologetics" (1997), http://www.ontruth.com/apologetics.html

196. Warfield, "Apologetics," n.p.

197. Bernard Kamm, *Varieties of Christian Apologetics* (Grand Rapids: Baker, 1961), 14-17.

198. John M. Frame, "Epistemological Perspectives and Evangelical Apologetics" (1982), http://www.frame-poythress.org/frame_articles/1982Epistemological.html

199. Frame, "Epistemological Perspectives," n.p

200. Montgomery, *Faith Founded on Fact*, xiv.

201.Cowan, Introduction to *Five Views*, 17.

202. Habermas, "Evidential Apologetics," 92.

203. Van Til, *Defense of the Faith*, 100.

204. Ibid.

205. Cowan, Introduction to *Five Views*, 19.

206. Van Til, *Defense of the Faith*, 179.

207. Ibid., 101

208. Montgomery, *Faith Founded on Fact,* ix.

209. Montgomery, *A History of Apologetics,* 17.

210. Cowan, Introduction to *Five Views,* 15ff.

211. William Lane Craig, "Classical Apologetics," in *Five Views on Apologetics,* ed. Steven B. Cowan (Grand Rapids: Zondervan, 2000), 48-49.

212. Cowan, Introduction to *Five Views,* 16.

213. Clifford, *Montgomery's Legal Apologetic,* 244.

214. Ibid., 246.

215. Ibid., 137.

216 Cowan, Introduction to *Five Views,* 17.

217. Basil Mitchell, *The Justification of Religious Belief* (New York: Oxford University Press, 1981), 35.

218. Paul D. Feinberg, "Cumulative Case Apologetics," in *Five Views on Apologetics,* ed. Steven B. Cowan (Grand Rapids: Zondervan, 2000), 151.

219. Ibid., 153-56.

220. Gary R. Habermas, "An Evidentialist's Response" (to Cumulative Case Apologetics), in *Five Views on Apologetics,* ed. Steven B. Cowan (Grand Rapids: Zondervan, 2000), 184.

221. Paul D. Feinberg, "A Cumulative Case Apologist's Response" (to Evidential Apologetics), in *Five Views on Apologetics,* ed. Steven B. Cowan (Grand Rapids: Zondervan, 2000), 129-31.

222. Cowan, Introduction to *Five Views,* 18.

223. Clifford, *Montgomery's Legal Apologetic,* 57.

224. Feinberg, "Cumulative Case Apologetics," 167.

225. Cited in Cowan, Introduction to *Five Views,* 19.

226. Ronald B. Mayers, *Balanced Apologetics: Using Evidences and Presuppositions in Defense of the Faith* (Grand Rapids: Kregel Publications, 1984), 197.

227. Mayers, *Balanced Apologetics,* 198.

228. Steven B. Cowan, Conclusion to *Five Views on Apologetics,* ed. Steven B. Cowan (Grand Rapids: Zondervan, 2000),.380-81.

229. Van Til, *Defense of the Faith,* 199.

230. Ibid., 180.

231. Ibid., 199.

232. John M, Frame, *Apologetics to the Glory of God: An Introduction* (Phillipsburg, NJ: Presbyterian and Reformed Publishing Company, 1994),.xi.

233. Ibid., xii.

234. Ibid., 9.

235. Ibid.

236. Gary R. Habermas, "An Evidentialist's Response" (to Presuppositional Apologetics), in *Five Views on Apologetics,* ed. Steven B. Cowan (Grand Rapids: Zondervan, 2000), 237.

237. Ibid.

238. Ibid., 247.

239. Clifford, *Montgomery's Legal Apologetic,* 150.

240. Peter Kreeft and Ronald K. Tacelli, *A Handbook of Christian Apologetics* (Downers Grove, IL: InterVarsity Press, 1994), 176ff.

241. Ibid., 181.

242. Ibid., 182.

243. Ibid.

244. Ibid.

245. Ibid., 195.

246. Habermas, "Jesus' Resurrection," 162.

247. Gary R. Habermas, "An Evidentialist's Response" (to Cumulative Case Apologetics), in *Five Views on Apologetics,* ed. Steven B. Cowan (Grand Rapids: Zondervan, 2000), 187.

248. Habermas, "Jesus' Resurrection" (Part II), 378.

249. Habermas, "Evidential Apologetics," 100-121.

250. Ibid., 92.

251. Ibid., 95.

252. Ibid., 107.

253. Ibid., 115.

254. Ibid., 119.

255. Habermas and Licona, *Case for the Resurrection,* 36-39.

256. Ibid., 33.

257. Ibid., 32.

258. Montgomery, *A History of Apologetics,* 13.

259. Dulles, *History of Apologetics,* xvi.

260. Van Til, *Defense of the Faith,*180.

261. Greg Bahnsen, "Evidential Apologetics: The Right Way" (1995), http://www.solagratia.org/ Articles/Evidential_Apologetics_The_Right_Way. aspx

262. Richard Packham, "Critique of John Warwick Montgomery's Arguments for the Legal Evidence for Christianity" (1998), http://www.infidels/modern/ richard_packham/montgmry.html.

263. Boyd Pehrson, "How Not to Critique Legal Apologetics," *Global Journal of Classical Theology*: *3*(1) (March, 2002).

264. Pinnock, *Set Forth Your Case,* 23ff.

265. Ibidl, 21.

266. Ibid., 27.

267. Ibid., 136.

268. Ibid., 54.

269. John Warwick Montgomery, *The Suicide of Christian Theology* (Newburgh, IN: Trinity Press, 1970), 8.

270. Ibid., 37.

271. Montgomery, *Faith Founded on Fact,*.38–39.

272. H. Wayne House and Joseph M. Holden, *Charts of Apologetics and Christian Evidences.* (Grand Rapids: Zondervan, 2006), 9.

273. Feinberg, "Cumulative Case Apologetics," 169.

274. Ibid.

275. Ibid., 170.

276. Habermas, "An Evidentialist's Response (to Cumulative Case Apologetics), 191.

277 John M. Frame, "Presuppositionalist Apologetics," in *Five Views on Apologetics,* ed. Steven B. Cowan (Grand Rapids: Zondervan, 2000), 226.

278. Teh, "Legal Apologetics," n.p.

279. Clifford, *Montgomery's Legal Apologetic,* 238.

280. Ibid., 239.

281. Montgomery, *The Law above the Law*, 85.

282. Clifford, *Montgomery's Legal Apologetic*, 247.

283. Francis Beckwith, *David Hume's Argument Against Miracles: A Critical Analysis* (New York: University Press of America, 1989), 122.

284. Johnson, "Juridical Apologetics," 1.

285. Montgomery, *The Law above the Law*, 86.

286. Clifford, *Montgomery's Legal Apologetic*, 238-39.

287. Ibid., 243.

288. Montgomery, *The Law above the Law*, 86.

289. Clifford, *Montgomery's Legal Apologetic*, 240.

290. Montgomery, *The Law above the Law*, 89-90.

291. C. Stephen Evans. *Why Believe?* (Leicester, UK: InterVarsity, 1996), 10ff.

292. Clifford, *Montgomery's Legal Apologetic*, 244.

293. Ibid., 46.

294. Packham, "Critique of Montgomery's Arguments," n.p.

295. Ibid.

296 Pehrson, "How Not to Critique Legal Apologetics," n.p.

297. James Patrick Holding, "First of All, Let's Laugh at All the Lawyers," http://tektoinics.org/lp/packham/1.html.

298. John M. Frame, "A Presuppositionalist's Response" (to Evidential Apologetics), in *Five Views on Apologetics,* ed. Steven B. Cowan (Grand Rapids: Zondervan, 2000), 137.

299. Habermas and Licona, *Case for the Resurrection,* 33.

300. Habermas, "Jesus' Resurrection,".385.

Works Cited

Althaus, Paul. *The So-Called Kerygma and the Historical Jesus*. Translated by David Cairns. London: Oliver & Boyd. 1959.

Anderson, Robert. *A Doubter's Doubts about Science and Religion*. 3rd Ed. Glasgow: Pickering & Inglis, 1924.

Aquinas, Thomas. *Summa contra Gentiles*: *Book Three: Providence, Part 1*. Translated by Vernon J. Bourke. Notre Dame, IN: University of Notre Dame Press, 1975.

Bahnsen, Greg. "Evidential Apologetics: The Right Way," 1995. http://www.solagratia. org/Articles/Evidential_Apologetics_The_ Right_Way.aspx

Barth, Karl. *Church Dogmatics*. Edited by G. W. Bromley and T. F. Torrance. Edinburgh: T & T Clark, 1956.

Beckwith, Francis. *David Hume's Argument Against Miracles: A Critical Analysis*. New York: University Press of America, 1989.

Black, C. Clifton. *The Rhetoric of the Gospel: Theological Artistry in the Gospels and Acts*. St. Louis: Chalice, 2001.

Boa, Kenneth D., and Robert M. Bowman. *Faith Has Its Reasons: An Integrative Approach to Defending Christianity*. Colorado Springs: NavPress, 2001.

Butler, Joseph. *The Analogy of Religion Natural and Revealed to the Constitution and Course of Nature*. 1736. Reprint, New York: Ungar, 1961.

Bultmann, Rudolph. *Kerygma and Myth: A Theological Debate*. Translated by R. H. Fuller. London: Austin Farrer, 1953.

— — —. *Theology of the New Testament*. Translated by K Goebel. New York: Scribner's, 1951.

Carnell, Edward John. *Introduction to Christian Apologetics*. Grand Rapids: Eerdmans, 1948.

Carrigan, Cky J. "Contemporary Evangelical Approaches to Apologetics" (1997). http://www.ontruth.com/apologetics.html

Cavin, Robert Gregg. "Is There Sufficient Historical Evidence to Establish the Resurrection of Jesus?" *Faith and Philosophy* *12*(3)(July, 1995): 361-79.

Chandler, Walter. *The Trial of Jesus from a Lawyer's Standpoint*. New York: Federal Press, 1925.

Chrispin, Gerard. *The Resurrection: The Unopened Gift*. Epson, Surrey: Day One Publications, 1999.

Clifford, Ross. *John Warwick Montgomery's Legal Apologetic: An Apologetic for All Seasons*. Bonn: Verlag for Kultur und Wissenschaft, 2004.

Cowan, Steven B. "Conclusion." In *Five Views on Apologetics,* 375-81. Edited by Steven B. Cowan. Grand Rapids: Zondervan, 2000.

———. "Introduction." In *Five Views on Apologetics,* 7-20. Edited by Steven B. Cowan. Grand Rapids: Zondervan, 2000.

Craig, William Lane. "Classical Apologetics." In *Five Views on Apologetics*, 26-55. Edited by Steven B. Cowan. Grand Rapids: Zondervan, 2000.

— — —. *The Historical Argument for the Resurrection of Jesus During the Deist Controversy.* Lewiston: Edwin Mellen, 1985.

Derret, J. Duncan M. *Law in the New Testament.* London: Durton, Longman, and Todd, 1970.

Dulles, Avery. *A History of Apologetics.* 1971. Reprint, Eugene, OR: Wipf and Stock, 1999.

Dyrness, William. *Christian Apologetics in a World Community.* Downers Grove, IL: InterVarsity, 1983.

Evans, C. Stephen. *Why Believe?* Leicester, UK: InterVarsity, 1996.

Feinberg, Paul D. "A Cumulative Case Apologist's Response" (to Evidential Apologetics). In *Five Views on Apologetics,* 129-31. Edited by Steven B. Cowan. Grand Rapids: Zondervan, 2000.

— — —. "Cumulative Case Apologetics" In *Five Views on Apologetics,* 148-72. Edited by.Steven B. Cowan. Grand Rapids: Zondervan, 2000.

Frame, John M. "A Presuppositionalist's Response" (to Evidential Apologetics). In *Five Views on Apologetics,* 132-37. Edited by Steven B. Cowan. Grand Rapids: Zondervan, 2000.

———. *Apologetics to the Glory of God: An Introduction*. Phillipsburg, NJ: Presbyterian and Reformed Publishing Company, 1994.

———. Epistemological Perspectives and Evangelical Apologetics. 1982. http://www.frame-poythress.org/frame_articles/1982Epistemological.html

———. "Presuppositionalist Apologetics." In *Five Views on Apologetics*, 208-31. Edited by Steven B. Cowan. Grand Rapids: Zondervan, 2000.

Greenleaf, Simon. *The Testimony of the Evangelists: The Gospels Examined by the Rules of Evidence*. Grand Rapids: Kregel Classics, 1995.

Grotius, Hugo. *The Truth of the Christian Religion*. Translated by John Clarke. Whitefish, MT: Kessinger Publishing, 2004.

Habermas, Gary R. "An Evidentialist's Response" (to Cumulative Case Apologetics.) In *Five Views on Apologetics*, 184-93. Edited by Steven B. Cowan. Grand Rapids: Zondervan, 2000.

———. "An Evidentialist's Response" (to Presuppositional Apologetics). In *Five Views on Apologetics*, 236-48. Edited by Steven B. Cowan. Grand Rapids: Zondervan, 2000.

— — —. "Evidential Apologetics." In *Five Views on Apologetics*, 92-121. Edited by Steven B. Cowan. Grand Rapids: Zondervan, 2000.

— — —. "Greg Bahnsen, John Warwick Montgomery, and Evidential Apologetics." *Global Journal of Classical Theology:* 3(1) (March, 2002).

— — —. "Jesus' Resurrection and Contemporary Criticism: An Apologetic." *Criswell Theological Review*: 4(1) (1989): 159-74.

— — —. "Jesus' Resurrection and Contemporary Criticism: An Apologetic" (Part II). *Criswell Theological Review*: 4(2) (1990): 373-85.

Habermas, Gary R., and Michael R. Licona. *The Case for the Resurrection of Jesus*. Grand Rapids: Kregel Publications, 2004.

Hazen, Craig. "Ever Hearing but Never Understanding: A Response to Mark Hutchins's Critique of John Warwick Montgomery's Historical Apologetics." *Global Journal of Classical Theology*: 3(1) (March, 2002).

Hoffecker, N. Andrew. "Augustine, Aquinas and the Reformers." In *Building a Christian World View: Volume 1, God, Man and Knowledge*, 235-58. Edited by W. Andrew Hoffecker and Gary Scott Smith. Phillipsburg, NJ: Presbyterian and Reform Publishing, 1986.

Holding, James Patrick. "First of All, Let's Laugh at All the Lawyers." http://tektoinics.org/lp/packham)1.html.

House, H. Wayne, and Joseph M. Holden, *Charts of Apologetics and Christian Evidences*. Grand Rapids: Zondervan, 2006.

Johnson, Phillip. "Juridical Apologetics 1600-2000 AD: A Bio-Bibliographical Essay." *Global Journal of Classical Theology*: 3(1) (March 2002), 1-25.

Kamm, Bernard. *Varieties of Christian Apologetics*. Grand Rapids: Baker, 1961.

Kierkegaard, Soren. *On Authority and Revelation*. Translated by Walter Lowrie. Princeton: Princeton University Press, 1955.

— — —. *Philosophical Fragments*. Translated by D. F. Swenson. Princeton: Princeton University Press, 1941.

Kreeft, Peter, and Ronald K. Tacelli. *A Handbook of Christian Apologetics*. Downers Grove, IL: InterVarsity Press, 1994.

Lamb, Francis J. *Miracle and Science: Biblical Miracles Examined by the Methods, Rules, and Tests of the Science of Jurisprudence* as *Administered Today in Courts of Justice.* Oberlin, OH: Bibliotheca Sacra, 1909.

Linton, Irwin H. *A Lawyer Examines the Bible: An Introduction to Christian Evidences.* 5th Ed. Boston: W. A. Wilde, 1943.

Mayers, Ronald B. *Balanced Apologetics: Using Evidences and Presuppositions in Defense of the Faith.* Grand Rapids: Kregel Publications, 1984.

McGrath, Allister E. "Apologetics to the Romans." *Bibliotheca Sacra*: *155* (October-December, 1998), 387-93.

McRoberts, Kerry D. "Faith Founded on Fact: The Apologetic Theology of John Warwick Montgomery." Master's Thesis, Regent College, 1998.

Mitchell, Basil. *The Justification of Religious Belief.* New York: Oxford University Press, 1981.

Montgomery, John Warwick. *Faith Founded on Fact: Essays in Evidential Apologetics.* Newburgh, IN: Trinity College and Seminary, 1978.

———. *History and Christianity: A Vigorous, Convincing Presentation of the Evidence for a Historical Jesus.* Minneapolis: Bethany House, 1964.

— — —. *A History of Apologetics through the Centuries.* Newburgh, IN: Trinity College and Seminary, n.d

— — —. *Human Rights and Human Dignity.* Grand Rapids: Zondervan, 1986.

— — —. "The Jury Returns: A Juridical Defense of Christianity." In *Christians in the Public Square,* 223-50. Edited by C.E.B. Cranfield, David Kilgour, and John Warwick Montgomery Edmonton, AB: Canadian Institute for Law, Theology and Public Policy, 1996.

— — —. "The Jury Returns: A Juridical Defense of Christianity." In *Evidence for Faith: Deciding the God Question,* 319-41. Edited by John Warwick Montgomery. Edmonton, AB: Canadian Institute for Law, Theology and Public Policy, 2004.

— — —. *The Law above the Law. Why the Law Needs Biblical Foundations/How Legal Thought Supports Christian Truth.* Minneapolis: Bethany House, 1975.

— — —. "Neglected Apologetic Styles: The Juridical and the Literary." In *Evangelical Apologetics,* 119-33. Edited by Michael Bauman, David Hall, and Robert Newman. Camp Hill: PA: Christian Publications, 1996.

———, *The Suicide of Christian Theology.* Newburgh, IN: Trinity Press, 1970.

———. *A History of Apologetics through the Centuries.* Newburgh, IN: Trinity College and Seminary, n.d

Morrison, Charles R. *Proofs of Christ's Resurrection from a Lawyer's Standpoint.* Andover: Warren F. Draper, 1882.

Origen. *Origen Contra Celsum.* Translated by Henry Chadwick. Second edition. Cambridge: University Press, 1965).

Packham, Richard. "Critique of John Warwick Montgomery's Arguments for the Legal Evidence for Christianity." (1998) http://www.infidels/modern/richard_packham/montgmry.html.

Paley, William. *A View of the Evidences of Christianity.* 1794. Reprint, London: Longmans, 1830.

Pascal, Blaise. *Pensees.* Translated by A. J. Krailsheimer. Revised edition. London: Penguin Books, 1995.

Pehrson, Boyd. "How Not to Critique Legal Apologetics." *Global Journal of Classical Theology*: 3(1) (March 2002). http://www.trinitysem.edu/journal/pehrsonpap.html.

Pinnock, Clark H. *Set Forth Your Case: An Examination of Christianity's Credentials.* Chicago: Moody, 1967.

Reimarus, Herman S. "Concerning the Intention of Jesus and His Teachings" In *Reimarus Fragments.* Edited by Charles H. Talbert. Translated by Ralph S. Fraser. London: SCN, 1971.

Russell, Howard Hyde. *A Lawyer's Examination of the Bible.* Westerville, OH: Bond, 1935.

Sagebeer, Joseph Evans. *The Bible in Court.* Philadelphia: Lippincott, 1900.

Sherlock, Thomas. *The Tryal of the Witnesses of the Resurrection of Jesus.* London: J. Roberts, 1729.

— — —. *The Tryal of the Witnesses of the Resurrection of Jesus.* In *Jurisprudence: A Book of Readings,* 339-450. Edited by John Warwick Montgomery. Strasbourg: International Scholarly Publications, 1974.

Sperry, Willard. *"Yes, But—." The Bankruptcy of Apologetics.* New York: Harper, 1931.

Strauss, David Friedrich. *Life of Jesus.* Translated by George Eliot. London, 1846.

Teh, Henry Hock Guan. "Legal Apologetics: Principles of Legal Evidence as Applied to the Quest for Religious Truth." *Global Journal of Classical* Theology: 5(1) (July 2005).

Tertullian. *Apology.* Translated by Emily Joseph Daly. New York: Fathers of the Church Inc., 1950.

Trites, Allison. *The New Testament Concept of Witness.* Cambridge: Cambridge University Press, 1977.

Van Til, Cornelius. *The Defense of the Faith.* Phillipsburg, NJ: Presbyterian and Reformed Publishing, 1955.

Warfield. Benjamin B. "Apologetics." http://www/reformed.org/apologetics/index.html.

Wharton, Francis. "Recent Changes in Jurisprudence and Apologetics." *The Princeton Review*: 2(1) (July-December, 1878): 139-52.

Williams, Stephen. *The Bible in Court or Truth v. Error.* Dearborn, MI: Dearborn Press, 1925.

Winter, Bruce W. "Official Proceedings and Forensic Speeches in Acts 24-26." In *The Book of Acts in Its Ancient Literary Settings*, 305-36. Edited by Bruce W. Winter and Andrew D. Clarke. Grand Rapids: Eerdmans, 1994.

Printed in the United States
152865LV00001BA/1/P

9 781607 919681